KŪHAKU & OTHER ACCOUNTS FROM JAPAN

KŪHAKU.

OTHER ACCOUNTS FROM JAPAN

(over 10 pages of illustrations!)

CHIN MUSIC PRESS – *PUBLISHERS*

CHIN MUSIC PRESS INC.
2621 24th Ave. w
Seattle, WA 98199
USA.

http://www.chinmusicpress.com

First edition

Designed by Craig Mod
Printed in Iceland by Oddi Printing*
*Printing decision was in no way influenced by
our love of Bjork, Halldor Laxness (*Independent
People* is sheer brilliance) or the way the word
"Reykjavik" trips off the tongue.

Kūhaku
& Other Accounts from Japan
ISBN 0-9741995-0-8

"Groped" by Sharon Moshavi was
adapted from an October 31, 2002,
radio broadcast on National Public
Radio entitled "Breaking the Public
Anger Taboo in Japan."

All three parts of "That Floating
Feeling" by Sumie Kawakami were
excerpted and translated from the
book *Tsuma no Koi: Tatoe Furin to
Yobarete mo* (Wives in Love: Even if
it's Called Immoral) ISBN:4-901203-
24-X, Astra Inc. July 2004.

"Father Hunters" by Roland Kelts
was originally published in the
spring 2000 edition of *DoubleTake*
magazine. This version of the article
has been updated.

"Garbage" by Sharon Moshavi
originally appeared as "Deciphering
Japan's Trash Codes." Copyright
2002, *International Herald Tribune*.
Reprinted by permission.

Canned coffee artwork produced
with the permission of Asahi Soft
Drinks Co. (Wonda Morning Shot),
Japan Tobacco Inc. (Roots Real
Blend) and Nestle Japan Group
(Santa Marta X).

Definition of *kūhaku* taken in part
from *Kenkyusha's New Japanese-
English Dictionary*.

Parts of this book are intended to be
read aloud onstage to the honk and
twitter of a saxophone.

"When I think how I have been swindled by books of Oriental travel, I want a tourist for breakfast."

— *Mark Twain*
The Innocents Abroad

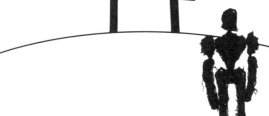

CONTENTS

Preface

Glossary

In September 2002, I was stuck in traffic in the cramped back seat of a Benz 190 on a grey day along a very grey stretch of highway heading toward Hakone. We were going to Fuji Reien, a sprawling graveyard at the base of Mount Fuji, where I was to represent the family at a ceremony for my late father-in-law. My wife, Yuko, was in Seattle, pregnant and unable to make the trip back to Japan, so I was sent to say a few words in my most polite Japanese, slip an envelope thick with ten-thousand yen notes into the priest's hands and pass out gifts to the few relatives in attendance.

In the back seat of that Benz, as my late mother-in-law's sister plied me with convenience-store sandwiches, canned coffee and snacks, I reflected on the decade and a half I had spent in Japan. I met my wife here, became a father, had wonderful times with her parents before they died. Japan is where I played softball and baseball – not well, but with religious zeal. It's where I was forced to sing karaoke. It's where I taught at prestigious universities, edited a weekly newspaper and a monthly magazine, wrote a book and also suffered through some of the most mind-numbing translation and proofreading jobs imaginable. It's where I drank with low-level gangsters, soaked in outdoor baths in the snow, crashed Akira Kurosawa's birthday party and had my lip go numb with blowfish venom.

While the Benz inched along in bumper-to-bumper traffic on the Tomei Expressway, I began to envision a book of essays about my time in Japan. But later, I rejected that idea. It's been done to death, I thought. We've had James Fallows and Lafcadio Hearn present their takes on Japan. Who needs the views of another lanky Westerner?

But what if I brought together a group of writers – a mix of Westerners and Japanese – who probably wouldn't even get along if they were stuck in the same room? What if the stories focused on how things are, not as yet another Westerner thinks they should be? Reportage trumping armchair analysis, I thought as we traveled toward the cemetery.

Those fleeting thoughts on that grey highway were the seeds that grew into this imperfect, democratic book. They also are the reason I founded Chin Music Press in October 2002. It seemed to me at the time – and still makes sense today, I might add – that as media conglomerates expand faster than Violet Beauregarde in *Charlie and the Chocolate Factory*, they are giving small publishers an opportunity. We can present books that are difficult to categorize but fun to read – something they are increasingly unwilling to do these days because of their obsession with the bottom line.

Most people hear "small publisher" and think "obscure poetry" or "impenetrable fiction." We're out to change that image. Chin Music Press gets its name - and its mission - from the varied meanings of the phrase "chin music." It's a quintessentially American phrase, tied as it is to baseball and to a folksy description of spoken language. Mark Twain used the phrase in 1872 in *Roughing It*. Flapper girls in the Roaring Twenties used it as a synonym for gossip. In 1921, H.L. Mencken included it in his book *The American Language* as an example of "the racy neologisms of American." And it's still heard today from baseball announcers - although not as often as we'd like - when a pitcher like Kerry Wood throws one of those high-and-tight fastballs that is meant to tell the batter: "Next time, it's your noggin."

Kūhaku and Other Accounts from Japan reflects our approach to publishing. It's part aggressive chatter, part gossip and part the literary equivalent of a knockdown pitch.

Finally, I'd like to thank the following people: Craig Mod, a talented young designer who understands the importance of bringing beautiful things into this world; Yuko Enomoto, my guiding light; David Cady, a sharp editor who never wavered in support of this project and injected a playful touch into these pages; J. Mark Lytle for his advice, editorial insights and friendship; all the writers, who put up with shifting deadlines and a publishing team that was learning on the fly; David Rutledge for his helpful comments; Kaori Funabiki for her patience; Kimiko, Kate and Kenzo for (usually) playing quietly behind me as I edited; the talented artists kozyndan and Peyote; Roland Kelts for his invaluable guidance in the ways of the publishing world; Hiroshi "Day" Inoshita, for teaching me the fundamentals of this trade; and, of course, mom and dad, for, among other things, making me.

Bruce Rutledge
March 9, 2004
Seattle, USA

PLACES *KŌHAKU* WAS MADE:
Starbucks, *Ebisu*
Some small coffee joint in *Ebisu*
Kouhei's room, *Ebisu*
Starbucks, *Jimbocho*
A totally wacky (but very delicious) Russian restaurant, *Jimbocho*
The office of the super-nice Mr. Otobe, *Jimbocho*
Apartment Cafe, *Koenji*
Mister Donut, *Nishikasai*
Drew's pad, *Nishikasai*
Satoko's house, *Nishi Waseda*
Panama Hotel, *Seattle*
Chin Music Press headquarters, also known as that room next to the playroom, *Seattle*
On long walks through Elliot Bay Park, *Seattle*
David Cady's house in Ballard, *Seattle*
Magnolia Appassionato, *Seattle*
Vox House, *Takada*
Starbucks, *Takadanobaba*
Ben's Cafe, *Takadanobaba*
Place, *Takadanobaba*
Mister Donut, *Takadanobaba*
New Yorker's Cafe, *Takadanobaba*
Excelsior Cafe, *Takadanobaba*
While riding the Tozai, Hibiya and Yamanote lines
Denny's on *Shinmejiro-Dori*
Tokyo immigration office, *Shinagawa*

GROPED
sharon moshavi

I BEAT UP A JAPANESE BUSINESSMAN recently. Beat him silly. Pummeled him senseless, leaving him stunned in the middle of a busy Tokyo intersection.

Allow me to explain. He had it coming, you see. I was on my way home after an evening out with friends and was standing on a corner, waiting for the light to change. He appeared at my side, a drunken fifty-something businessman, with dark grey hair and a light grey suit. His fogged eyes looked toward me and he muttered something incomprehensible. Then, without any warning, he reached out and grabbed my left breast. Just grabbed it.

I think I froze in shock for a moment, but then another instinct took over, and I smacked him with the flat of my hand. Then I did it again, and again. He just stood there, with bloodshot, drunken eyes. I got even angrier. I kept hitting him. He didn't try to leave; he simply held up a shopping bag to defend himself from my blows. I grabbed the bag and beat him with that. Until the bag broke. Dozens of pieces of paper floated to the ground. He reached down into the street to pick them up, and I used that opportunity to kick him.

Someone shouted at me in English, and I looked up to realize a crowd had gathered around us, and traffic had stopped. It was as if I'd emerged from a trance. What had I just done? Dazed and bewildered, I fled.

I've since told this tale to a number of friends here. The women are impressed and awed. The men look a bit scared. Frankly, I'm a bit scared myself. Where in the world did all that anger come from?

At first I thought it was simply because I've been groped so often. I travel a lot, and one of the consequences of being an independent female traveler is that a few unwanted hands come your way. I've been pawed and pinched from India to Indonesia. A single thump to the back of a fleeing groper is the only revenge I'd ever managed to exact.

But I think there is another reason why I exploded like a

bottle of warm seltzer. I think I was so angry because in Japan I just don't have much opportunity to get angry. People just don't do it. Yelling and anger are considered immature. I never have the kind of heated encounters, even tiny ones, I'm used to having in the US and most everywhere else. Everything's calm; everyone's calm. This place will knock a few points off anyone's blood pressure.

But it's killing me. I don't think it's good for the soul to be so even-tempered. Life demands upheaval, tempestuousness. Every once in a while, I need to exchange a few snide words with a telephone sales representative or a cable repairman. A bit of bickering gets my adrenalin pumping. Besides, anger can be a safety valve, a ventilation system that cools down violence. Express enough anger in your life, and it might prevent you from doing something you regret, like attacking a pathetic Japanese salaryman.

To make sure I don't become a vessel of repression again and maul someone else, I'm determined to insert a little more conflict into my life. I started the other day at my bank in Tokyo. I was having a problem there, and the bank of course was totally in the wrong, but the manager refused to budge. She also refused to get angry. So I stood there, for forty-five minutes, trying to rile her. I failed. She didn't even ask me to leave. She just stood there and patiently explained the situation.

I finally stormed out. I was furious. As the anger coursed through me, I felt wonderful, exuberant. And I didn't even have to lay a finger on her.

THAT FLOATING FEELING I

sumie kawakami
translation by yuko enomoto

Chieko Hamuro is a thirty-three-year-old homemaker in Tokyo.
She was interviewed in her home in June 2003.

M Y OLDEST DAUGHTER, who turned five this year, is into TV shows about animals – shows about sea turtles risking their lives to lay their eggs on land, a lioness teaching its cubs how to hunt, a kangaroo breastfeeding its offspring in her pouch. She'll say, "Mom, look! A giraffe!"

When my three-year-old rests his head on my lap as we sit on the sofa, my daughter approaches from the other side and rests her head on my shoulder. This moment – when I feel the warmth of my children as we sit down to watch TV shows about animals – is one of pure relaxation. For some people, it may even be a picture of true happiness. But as I watch these shows – with all the animals fighting the elements to raise their offspring – I begin to feel anxious.

For example, if I were attacked by a bear in a forest, would I be able to fight it and protect my children? Of course, I love my children unconditionally, and I know that if for some ultimate reason I had to risk my own life to save my children's, I would die for them, although perhaps not gladly. But that's an obligation; I don't feel as if it's true love. When I think of these things, I am pained to think that I may be lacking in love.

But then I'll catch myself. Why am I thinking about bears in the first place? I am at home, watching TV. There's absolutely no possibility of a bear attack. And although violent crimes are on the rise, the possibility of an armed gunman suddenly breaking into our house is almost the same as getting hit by a car just walking down the street. Even then, these feelings of insecurity, these "what ifs," plague me constantly, leaving me feeling like I'm in a battered old airplane, flying through thick rain clouds and staying just barely above the ground.

"It's because the children are so young," my husband told me. I do tend to over-analyze. The doctor calls it "a mild anxiety," so when I remember, I try to go in for visits. Is this really anxiety? Where does it end?

I have gotten better lately.

People say a woman gains confidence in herself when she gives birth and becomes a mother. But for me, it was the complete opposite. From the time I found out that I was expecting to the time I gave birth, there was not a single day of joy; it was dominated by morning sickness, bloating, pain in my breasts, never-ending, low-grade fevers. The only reason I had the child is because I was pregnant … A month before I conceived, my husband was unemployed because the foreign firm he worked for had closed its office. I wanted to work, but I couldn't get an abortion. My husband really wanted this child.

I became pregnant six months after we got married. I can't help but feel like I had been set up, like he was purposely not being careful.

That day, my husband was reading *National Geographic* or something like that, and he said to me, "They say the chances for male births are higher during wartime." According to the article, there is a correlation between male births and stressful conditions surrounding a pregnancy. Because male mortality rates increase during a war, more boys are born.

"It's about preservation of the species," he said. "They say people are more likely to have sex during extreme conditions, such as war. If death were inevitable, one would be driven to leave behind a child or two. That's male instinct."

My husband sounded as if he had just attained enlightenment. That probably was the day I got pregnant.

This might sound as if I have no maternal instinct, but I can never trust a woman who says, "I am happy as long as I have my husband and children. I can overcome any hardship." Saying you can't work because you have children is a good excuse, but when I see lazy housewives taking advantage of that, I get angry. Perhaps it only looks that way because of my own frustration with raising children. The reason I started seeing someone was partly due to this frustration, in addition to hormonal imbalances.

When I look back on those times, I realize I was over-reacting and thinking too much about work. My husband and I met at work, so I changed jobs after we got married. *(An unwritten code of the Japanese workplace is that a husband and wife should not work in the same office. And it's always the wife who has to go.)* When I got pregnant, I had been working for just six months in the research division of a securities firm. Having children was something for the future. I was shocked.

I mentioned that my husband was unemployed when I got pregnant. I wanted to be recognized at work. I didn't tell the company about my pregnancy because I didn't want to deal with my male colleagues and my boss. There were times when I got so depressed thinking about my expanding belly that I tore up my bedding and cried.

Times may have changed. But back then, foreign securities firms were magnets for women in search of blue-eyed, rich men. Some of these women eventually became specialists. Those who did were treated as equals of the men and were expected to behave as such. It was a workplace that recognized hard work. I believed it was a good place to start a career, which is why my pregnancy eventually made me angry. I unleashed that anger on my husband.

Specialists may say that I was experiencing maternity blues. Whatever the medical explanation, it doesn't change the fact that I was unhappy throughout pregnancy and childbirth – the supposedly rewarding moments of a woman's life.

Perhaps sensing a crisis, my husband found work a month later, and life settled into a routine. I could have continued working, but I was not feeling well. I had lost my fighting spirit and realized that I would rather quit than do a half-baked job at work. I was also turned off by the fact that my husband and I were in the same industry. No matter how hard I worked, I would never achieve the same status as my husband as long as we had children; that led me to a feeling of desperation, which gave way to a feeling like I had to even things out – he would have to take care of me to make up for this.

To maintain some rhythm in my life after I quit work, I commuted every day to a local library two train stops away. It kept me from thinking too much. The distance of thirty to forty minutes from home was good exercise and gave me a chance to read material other than work-related stuff. It had been a long time since I had read for fun, and I plunged into it, reading all sorts of books.

One day while I was reading, a foreign man came up to me and said, "You are always just reading." This American man, Andy, was working on his doctorate in Asian history and was here on a scholarship for research. His Japanese was perfect, and he enjoyed discussing literature. In time, I started seeing Andy a few days a week.

I told him about my pregnancy right away. It was hard to hide it as my belly was getting noticeably larger. I never expected this to become an intimate relationship, and I'm sure he didn't either. Andy had been married to a Japanese woman in the US but had divorced three years earlier. Maybe because of that, he had a sympathetic ear and listened while I told him about my faltering relationship with my husband in the wake of my pregnancy. At the time I was helplessly depressed.

One day, while walking through a park, I said, "I can't stand the way my body is becoming ugly. I don't want a baby." I cried. Andy stopped, held my shoulder and said, "Don't say that. You are very sexy, and the baby is sure to be proud of a mother like you."

I buried my face in his chest and cried. I didn't care that there were people around me.

"Then take me."

I remember thinking to myself, "What am I saying?" But I couldn't stop.

"Chie, you shouldn't say that," Andy said as he stepped away from me. "What about your husband?"

I didn't flinch. I squeezed his hand.

Andy was very gentle. He would put his face right up to my big belly and softly kiss it over and over. Sometimes during sex, the baby would move. "Come out soon," he would say.

My tryst with Andy lasted until he left, with the exception of one month before and after the birth. I would strap the newborn baby to my back and take the train to his apartment, wait until she napped, then make love with him.

I was breastfeeding my daughter, so my breasts were swollen. There were times when my daughter woke up; I would change her diaper while we were making love. But these things never seemed to bother Andy. It felt normal for me, too.

At times, I wondered if I had gone insane. This may sound strange, but my relationship with Andy was purely physical. He always told me I was sexy and that alone was enough for me. We never discussed our future. He was loving toward my daughter. Sometimes, he would lift her up and say, "I've known your mommy since you were in her belly."

He was a very understanding man. I never gave Andy my home phone number because I was afraid my husband would find out. I always initiated our contact. Andy never complained about the fact that he had no way of contacting me.

Looking back, I don't think it would be an overstatement to say Andy helped me get through the rough patches of my pregnancy and childbirth. That doesn't mean my husband was indifferent toward me and my daughter. Ever since I quit work, he did his very best to raise my battered spirit.

I was at my worst emotional state around the time I first met Andy. One time, I was just washing dishes and suddenly, I broke down crying and couldn't stop. I didn't see it coming. I didn't even feel like it was happening to me, and I couldn't figure out why I was crying.

My husband carried me to bed, tucked me in and sang me lullabies. Nobody's ever been this kind to me in adulthood. That, compounded by my feelings of guilt for betraying him, made me cry even more. That evening, he didn't ask any questions. He just stayed by my side until I fell asleep.

When our daughter was born, my husband thanked me and cried. I'd never seen him cry so much. It made me forget about the twelve-hour labor I had just gone through. I pulled his head close to my bed and caressed him.

I clearly loved my husband; I couldn't understand why I betrayed him like that. Revenge was definitely a part of it. He can't be blamed for the fact that I quit work. But I do feel like I had been pressured into having a baby before I was emotionally ready for it.

The greatest loss for me was dropping out of the work force. We often hear mothers with newborn babies say, "I am so busy, I have no time to think." For me, being alone for what felt like an eternity with an infant was unbearably lonely. The hours I spent with Andy as a woman while my daughter napped was what helped me be a mother the rest of the time. At the same time, I felt guilty that I was doing what I was doing because I was not maternal enough.

Andy left Japan before my daughter started walking.

"I will miss you," he said in English to me and my daughter and gave her a kiss on the cheek. I didn't see him off at the airport. He said his friend was driving him there. Come to think of it, I knew nothing about what he studied at the university, who he hung out with and what sort of life he led outside of his apartment. I never even asked.

After Andy left, I felt like an imbecile. I was unable to get out of bed in the morning, just rolling around and too lazy to prepare meals. I would slap something together for my daughter, but beyond that I would go almost all day without eating. Even my husband got worried. "You're with a small child all day. You must be tired. I'll take care of her, so let's go somewhere." He took a week off from work and flew us to Okinawa.

The first day, my husband took care of our child as promised, and I took a walk on the beach. I brought a book with me but didn't even open it. I just stared at the ocean all day.

The next day, we all went to the same beach. It was a great place to play for my daughter, who was just beginning to walk. I watched as my husband and my daughter played where the water meets the sand. After a while, our daughter fell asleep in my husband's arms. We put a towel in the shade and lay her down. We lay down next to her.

"Okinawa has such blue skies," my husband said as he put one arm under my head. It was so sudden, I jerked my body a little. He pretended not to notice and held my head tightly. Come to think of it, I don't think I had spent time with my husband like this since we found out about my pregnancy. Maybe we had, but I have no recollection of it.

"Sometimes I have no idea what's on your mind. I guess it's the stress of raising a child, but I don't know how to help you, and you don't seem to want my help. If you would only ask me, I would gladly help. But when I'm near you, it is as if you're saying, 'Leave me alone, don't come near me.' So all I do is wonder if I'm also helpless, and time just keeps ticking away. In the meantime, you are drifting further and further away. I feel pathetic because I can't do anything about it. I don't know what to do."

It sounded as if he were talking to himself.

I was too shocked to respond. I realized for the very first time that I was so absorbed with myself and my daughter that I had hardly noticed him. Also, I needed his help, but denied it. Just as I was going to get up and say something, he climbed on top of me and put his lips on mine.

We spent that day on the beach playing and eating, as if nothing had happened. But a big change was taking place inside of me. I kept repeating to myself what my husband told me. I had never sought help from him, no matter how desperate. I suffered alone because I couldn't say, "Help me."

By the time our vacation ended, I was energized. The distance between my husband and I shrank. On the flight home, I talked about the child-raising blues, my loss of confidence as a woman, all sorts of things. My husband listened.

After returning from Okinawa, I saw a counselor once a week for six months. In those sessions, I explored my maternity blues and my intense fear of seeking help from others. I also found out that my problems probably had something to do with growing up with a "perfect mother" – she took care of household matters single-handedly. I put pressure on myself to do the same. My mother was actually a very strong and patient person. She died of an illness when I was in college, but she barely complained right up to the end.

I try to talk about these things as much as I can with my husband now. I try to tell him how devastated I was by my mother's death, and how I tried to be strong in front of my little brother, who was still in high school. Sometimes I cry when we talk. I've surprised myself with the amount of tears I shed. I barely cried when my mother died, so why am I crying so much now?

I believe my husband and I are here today because of what we went through together then. My husband is more open with me now because I have opened up to him as well. Soon after, I became pregnant with our second child. This time, I told him about all my insecurities. I felt like I was really sharing my joy and pain with him.

I didn't say a word about Andy. I have no intention of ever telling him. I was a horrible wife for maintaining that sort of relationship, regardless of my mental state. But I also believe that it was a path toward maturity for me, and, therefore, not a worthless experience.

If you ask me, "Would I be able to forgive him if he did the same to me?" I would probably respond, "Never." I don't think I could handle it. Sometimes I wonder if my husband knows. But he would never ask. It shall remain buried forever.

⟡

FATHER HUNTERS
roland kelts

I was walking home from an *izakaya* one autumn evening in Osaka a few years ago, dodging clutches of drunk-
en businessmen down a narrow side street. Across the
road, over the gleaming roofs of a line of stopped cabs, I suddenly glimpsed the jerky, bobbing bodies of what American
police would call an "altercation." I froze, partly because an early evening fistfight is so uncommon a sight on Japanese walk-
ways, but mostly because of the participants involved.

A beet-faced man in his fifties hovered over a figure ly-
ing prone on the pavement. His jacket lay on the ground, and
his button-down shirt blazed white beneath the surrounding
black-light neon signs. The man on the ground couldn't have
been much over twenty and was struggling to raise his head of
bright, magenta-dyed hair. Next to him lay his bicycle, its han-
dlebars askew and its front wheel pointed skyward.

Two other men attempted to restrain the older man, but
their efforts failed. He lunged forward and kicked the bicyclist,
who curled into a fetal position. The assailant uttered a stream
of terse, sharp-edged epithets as he kicked. A group of younger
passersby had gathered and began chastening the older man to
little effect. At last he stopped kicking and grabbed his jacket,
but he continued to unleash a flurry of harsh language at the
supine figure. His clenched face showed nothing but unadul-
terated disgust.

I would soon learn that such scenes of intergeneration-
al fury (although not the kind I had witnessed) occur often
enough in contemporary Japan to have their own shorthand
label. *Oyaji-gari*, loosely translated as "father-hunting," refers
to a very specific act of violence: gangs of young men attacking
a man who is middle-aged or older, often a businessman dod-
dering home drunk, and leaving him badly beaten in the street.
The gangs usually attack in the predawn hush of the dimly lit,
labyrinthine alleyways and back streets of Japan's major cities,
and they are rarely caught. Most attackers hail from the nation's
massive middle class. According to police reports, the most

common motive they offer under questioning is boredom.

¶ "The economic bubble burst," Japanese novelist Haruki Murakami told me in his Tokyo studio on a hot May afternoon shortly after his fiftieth birthday. "And now most young people hate my generation. They say, 'My father doesn't understand me, and I don't understand him.' There's no communication at all."

Murakami's popularity among readers half his age or younger is as notable as his lack of support from veteran Japanese literati. He has traveled widely, spending years at a time in Europe and America, and he writes about his native land almost as an outsider. His books feature unmoored characters in phantasmagoric, half-Westernized Japanese cities. Mass culture and a deep-seated loneliness uneasily coexist.

According to Murakami, his younger Japanese readers respond to what he calls a "feeling of insecurity in a world with no system or discipline," a kind of free-floating anomie that feels inevitable amid Japan's eerily sterile urban landscapes. But he seems pained when I ask him to characterize those readers. "If those kids feel that their fathers are absent and emotionally unreliable, and if they don't like their parents, I think it's because of the defeat of my generation and its economic priorities. But this also means the defeat of Japanese values. And that's very sad." His brow lowers as he pauses and carefully folds his hands. "My generation worked hard for fifty years, and all of a sudden, maybe what they achieved means nothing. Now those kids feel lost in their own country."

This last comment was peculiarly resonant for me, not only as an American overseas, but as a man who often feels at sea, even (and sometimes, especially) at home. My mother is a Japanese expatriate, rigidly formal at times, diligent, severe, but also unfailingly polite and gracious. My father is an American of Scottish ancestry who tends towards social exuberance; he is loving and lovable in large, loud doses. I have learned to act as a bridge between them, but aside from spanning the divides between their races, I lose what little sense of my self I have when I do.

¶ Feeling lost in my own country was part of what drove me away from it. I'd flown to Osaka from New York, where I'd spent the years of my post-collegiate life engaging in rapacious consumerism on a daily basis. An existence devoted to working and spending and an increasingly willful social exuberance felt just as increasingly pointless. My sense of a self-defining heritage of any sort was rapidly receding, and the then-incessant rhetoric of globalism made this feeling more intense.

Like most Westerners under thirty-five or so, I went to Japan disguised as an English teacher, spending my days with kids in stiff, high-collared blue uniforms, or men and women in starched blue suits and skirts. But the real reason I'd taken up residence halfway around the world had more to do with escape – and an obsession with my mother's homeland, particularly since the once distant and daunting threat to American supremacy seemed to be faltering.

Japan's economic woes commenced around 1990, and by the time I arrived for my third visit to the country, in 1998, signs of an encroaching recession were pervasive. Unemployment was higher than in the United States, at 4.9 percent, for the first time since the immediate postwar period. The homeless count in Osaka-Jo Koen, a vast park surrounding a sixteenth-century castle that symbolizes the city's merchant-class origins, rose from four-thousand to sixteen-thousand in the span of five months. Nose-diving property values in Tokyo's Ginza district, where acres were once hyperbolically said to be worth more than the entire continental United States, resulted in one real estate agency holding a Sunday lottery to fill its floors of vacant condos at drastically deflated prices.

Yet Japan was still largely moneyed and hyper-urban. The overcrowded restaurants and bars, crammed elevators and escalators in ten-story department stores, gleaming cars, brand-name clothing and accessories and pulsing neon gambling parlors beneath advert-blaring video screens made Manhattan seem downright placid by comparison.

Most notable to me amid the metropolitan throngs of consumers was the free-form wealth of Japan's middle-class youths – those who were attending or had attended traditional neighborhood high schools and who were blessed with the overwhelming generosity of their prosperous postwar parents. Adult Japanese generally have more money in their savings accounts than do the people of any other advanced nation, largely because Japanese consider it shameful to be in debt. Money in the bank – or in secure, low-interest post office accounts – is crucial to one's social status and peace of mind.

With a flat economy, many parents began dipping into their precious savings to sustain their children's nightclubbing and jet-setting lifestyles. In certain neighborhoods – Kyobashi and Amemura (American Village) in Osaka, and Shibuya and Harajuku in Tokyo – the super-stylish young ruled, especially after two or three in the afternoon, when the cafes start serving the pre-evening snack, a staple meal in Japan. They would cruise past in a pageant of color and sound: the girls in face-paint glitter sprinkled atop deep parlor tans, their hair dyed auburn or white or streaked with *obasan* grey, their platform boots (with soles six to eight inches thick) rising up their calves to their knees; the boys, also artificially tanned, looking gaunt by Western standards, their locks sometimes bleached or blonde-streaked, brown and teased out surfer-style, or else permed into elaborate Afros, their hands gripping guitar cases or skateboards or packs of Mild Seven cigarettes. To the chattering of Pachinko gambling emporiums, the prerecorded voices crying, "*Irrashaimase!*" and the video-game blasts and elevated train rattle that are the soundtrack of urban Japan, these kids added the shrieks, shouts and trills of their *keitai denwa*. The tiny cellphones are festooned with colored beads or cartoon figures. Their owners can surf the Internet on their miniature screens, download ring-melodies from last week's top forty, send and receive email, and even take snippets of digital video to transmit instantly to the impatient.

"These kids are amazing," said Rufus Wainwright, the uber-hip underground American singer/songwriter whose concert I had attended at the behest of a mutual New York friend. Seated next to me in a fourth-floor bar, Wainwright shook his head. "They've studied American fashions down to the minutest details, you know. They mix them all together, but they've got everything just right. It's almost *too* right."

At the time, the kids were sporting the perfectly fitted flannel shirts and torn jeans and Converse sneakers that were once the hallmark of America's grunge scene, born in the lower-middle classes of the Pacific Northwest. They revved and raced jacked-up, heavy-mufflered, neon-lit Toyotas down the empty strips between skyscrapers after midnight, rendering a kind of slick, high-tech version of Saturday nights in midsized American towns. They toted mini-disc players, mini-amps, shiny guitars and expensive bags: Louis Vuitton, Prada, Gucci.

Many of them can afford to go to London or Paris or New York if they want to, but quite a few of them no longer see the point in it. Astute retailers import every item they could possibly want. With the attentiveness to detail commonly attributed to Japanese aesthetics, teenagers tailor what the world offers to suit their own exacting desires.

The kids can also afford their perfection. Young Japanese in their teens and early twenties seek a kind of modified financial self-reliance, living rent-free at home but devoting little of their time or attentions there. Overworked, guilt-ridden parents dole out generous allowances, and many students take unskilled part-time jobs in the expanding service-based industries of Japan's convenience culture – working at twenty-four-hour quick-stop stores or fast-food counters after school. Jobs of a type the Japanese call *freeter*, an amalgamation of the English "freelance" and the German *arbeiter* (*arubaito* in Japanese), allow young workers to retain the power to choose where and when they work, as opposed to the so-called salarymen and office ladies whose lives are dictated and defined by loyalty to their employers. In some cases, they drop out of school altogether and work in illicit trades, selling drugs and their bodies.

¶ Mika and Mayumi are high school dropouts who begin most of their days around two or three in the afternoon and spend their nights cruising the streets of Amemura until dawn. Both girls are eighteen, the daughters of an insurance clerk and a banker and their housewives, members of Japan's massive and aging middle class of corporate workers.

They were sporting what had come to be called the *yamamba* or "witch-woman" look, a term originating in Japanese folktales about an ogress who threatens local villagers and eats their children. The media applied the label derisively to the artificially bronzed, big-booted and blond-haired mini-Amazons; but my friend Nanami, who introduced me to the girls, said that they adopted the moniker proudly.

Mika and Mayumi agreed. "Old people are afraid of us," Mika declared, whereupon both girls giggled – chirped, really – in a duet that seemed rehearsed, or at least honed by repetition. They left high school because of a teacher who, according to Mayumi, sometimes resorted to physical violence to punish them. She admitted that tardiness was a problem for her, but "the school was so boring and stupid. They teach the same old things, and the teachers don't care who we are as individuals."

Were their parents concerned? "Not really," says Mayumi. "My parents are divorced, and my mom is really lonely. She's glad I'm home more now, even though I only spend about one day a week with her. We go shopping together."

The girls were happy to recount recent purchases, running through the names of chic downtown boutiques and European brand names with obvious ease and affection. Both Mayumi and Mika supplemented their budgets by working as clerks for a convenience store chain called FamilyMart.

Did they have boyfriends? I wondered, instantly feeling aged. Mika wrinkled her nose at me, and Mayumi giggled again. "We have sex," Mika replied. "We have sex-friends." Then she peered down at my notepad. "Is this for an American fashion magazine?"

When I said no, both girls rapidly lost interest and animation, eyeing the passing crowds and thumbing their miniature phones in a subtle mime of distraction. Not an ambassador of "America" via fashion or popular culture, I was simply another nosy foreigner.

Before leaving the States, I had been told that as an American in Japan, I'd be stared at, alternatively fawned over and wondered at, feared, snickered at, admired and possibly envied. Singled out, in any case. But at least in the urban centers, most young Japanese either eyed me dismissively or ignored me completely. As a *gaijin*, or "outside person," I didn't even flicker across their cellphone screens.

This new indifference towards Americans separates this generation from that of their parents, many of whom seemed to embrace American culture, at least in spirit, almost indiscriminately. (Even now, older Japanese will earnestly ask me what Americans think of Japan, then tensely await my answer as though the reputation of an entire culture were at stake.)

One weekend night, a forty-something busker in an Osaka alleyway was playing blues on his electric guitar and raised his hand to stop me. When I told him I was an American, he smiled. "We Japanese like old America, fun America. Bring back Marilyn Monroe and Elvis and Michael Jackson," he said, conflating bygone eras with frothy charm. "Not so much guns. Not so much sad stuff of now."

The United States still inspires wonder in Japan, but our country is harder to romanticize amid the onslaught of reportage via satellite and the Internet, which often highlights the stark difference between the two cultures. Video from 1999's Columbine shootings in Colorado, for example, appeared on Japanese television hours after the event occurred. Perplexed, wide-eyed colleagues and students at the school where I was teaching peppered me with questions: Did every American student own a gun? Did I own a gun? Did I ever see anyone get shot? Minutes after the 9/11 attacks in New York and Washington – live video aired during the primetime news hour – concerned Japanese friends phoned my apartment to express sympathy and escalating alarm.

In the summer of 2001, when an unemployed drifter in his thirties walked into an Osaka elementary school and slashed eight children to death, the Japanese media framed the story as the latest and most sensational example of moral decay. It was Japan's first-ever school killing spree, and it prompted heated debates over increased security for children and psychological counseling for the mentally ill. But the deeper explanation for why such a violent act had occurred at all was not hard to infer – from the media reports, but especially on the streets. "It's finally happened," a college student in Tokyo said to me, his eyes narrowing in consternation. "We've become just like America."

"We still copy American ways – too much, even," Nanami mused after our chat with the two girls. "But the American idea of being a rebel, an individual against society, maybe it doesn't work so well here." She paused. "Japan is still a kind of family. No one wants to be outside of the family, so how can you be a rebel?"

¶ "To begin to understand Japan," I was told on my first night in Tokyo, "you must know *tatemae* and *honne*."

The speaker was a man in his mid-fifties, wearing a blue suit, his hair lightly oiled and precisely parted. He was one of several government officials lecturing thousands of foreigners, all of us fresh off the plane.

"*Tatemae* is Japanese public face," he said, then briefly demonstrated an array of traditional, embarrassment-saving rituals: the deferential bowing, the litany of apologies and polite banter. "*Honne* is" – and here he grimaced and pointed squarely at his nose, the Japanese gesture for indicating the self – "the private."

Japan's social codes are in some ways its most successful sociocultural export: By now everyone knows about the bows, the politeness, the tea ceremonies, the flower arrangements and the powdered geisha. Popular novels and movies now bathe the geisha and samurai traditions in a haze of Hollywood glamour and Hallmark nostalgia previously unthinkable in the land that gave birth to them.

But in a country with a population half that of the United States, in an area smaller and less hospitable than the state of California, the strict codification of public and private space is no minor concern. Honor and dignity may be sexy; practical need arising out of severe limitations may be more telling.

What I would soon discover after settling into my tatami-floored apartment was a culture in which such codes are being twisted, turned in on themselves and reconceived. Japanese youths are acting out a drama of disrespect and rebellion as precisely codified and orchestrated as their parents' conformity. They look and act punkish, cool and unassailable, but they do so in unison, creating a barrier between themselves and their seniors – and foreigners like me.

While outrageous youth fashions are nothing new in Japan, openly outrageous behavior is new, behavior that has surfaced in the years after the bubble burst. On subways, Japanese over thirty sit with their knees properly turned inward, taking as little space as possible and staring straight ahead. Younger

Japanese sprawl on the floor, devouring fast food and gabbing on their cellphones. On the sidewalks, the high-fashion young race past their elders, riding bikes, skateboards or scooters, or clomping on foot, often knocking into their elders and sneering in open annoyance. Late into the night, school-age loiterers sit on curbstones outside convenience stores, smoking cigarettes, playing music and uttering threatening epithets as they snicker at the mostly single male customers, many of whom fear *oyaji-gari*-style attacks.

¶ The post World War II generation, aided by an America keen to invest in a Pacific ally, came of age in the economic boom years of the 1970s and 1980s. They worked incredibly hard, so hard that Japan became the first country to diagnose *karoshi*, or "death from overwork."

Today the elderly are living longer, the birthrate is dropping, and women are opting for careers instead of child-rearing. And those who have kids have fewer of them, all in the name of freedom and the need for space – peculiarly American import concepts. The accumulated wealth of Japan's boomer population – today's mothers and fathers – means that parents are spending more money on fewer kids, even as they have less time with them.

But traditionally, Japanese parents indulge their children far past the point of what an American might call spoiling them. Amid the silence and stiff shoulders of a bullet-train car, for example, it is not unusual to observe the sudden outbursts of a tantrum-throwing child whose parents then proceed to buy everything in sight from the ever-present vendor's carts – ice creams, *bento* lunch boxes, crackers, cookies – without ever appearing to admonish, let alone punish, the child. Childhood is still viewed as a sacred time of near-absolute freedom, before the rigid codes, restraints and social demands of adulthood lock firmly into place.

During exchanges with store clerks, my foreignness is most evident in my self-conscious adherence to Japanese etiquette. While younger Japanese make their purchases with nary an acknowledgement of the other party, I reflexively bow, uttering "please" and "thank you" several times. Some clerks, usually those past thirty, smile approvingly at my formalities, however garbled my delivery, while others blatantly ignore me, hustling my purchases through the electronic scanners as though all my chatter was a simpering waste of time. My mother stressed the importance of politeness, even in the most minor of social encounters. But in her native country, my habits now seem naïve, outdated, even ridiculous. Teenage boys behind me often grin sarcastically, muttering about "the foolish foreigner" holding up the line; the irony of an overly polite New Yorker is lost on them.

¶ Daiki Terasawa, the senior supervisor of Osaka City's Board of Education, who is also the father of a son attending the University of Tokyo, ascribes the younger generation's mood to Japan's complete loss of national aspirations. "The young see no purpose," he says.

Terasawa is a lean, expressive man in his late fifties who senses an urgent need for an overhaul of the country's social, political and economic institutions that can begin only when contemporary Japanese discover who they are. "In some ways, Japan achieved its goals. We became rich – the number two economy in the world, sometimes even number one. But Japan is rich only in material goods. We've lost our identity."

Terasawa believes the Japanese have lost interest in broader social issues. "Today's Japanese have grown selfish. They say, 'It's not my business, so it's not my duty.' I think the collapse of family obligation is the reason, everyone living apart and alone."

Young Japanese men, who have watched their fathers

disappear, are hesitant to marry. Young women, who have seen their mothers' spirits atrophy in loveless marriages, prefer to stay single, shop and vacation overseas. Many in their late twenties and early thirties are trying to move out of single-parent households into single-occupancy apartments. The drop in marriages means fewer babies, fewer families.

"Parents want the schools to teach morals instead of doing so themselves, and then they complain to us when their kids are disciplined," says Terasawa. He shakes his head. "The kids leave school and take service jobs for money, and the real problem is that they don't learn skills. The quality of Japanese products is suffering already." Mikio Nakadoi, a teacher in Osaka who left the profession ten years ago, is not surprised. "Those kids arrived at school without their books. They had snacks and phones and computer games. They were completely isolated then – and they're even worse off today."

Hikikomori, or "socially withdrawn," is another term coined to label a generation of kids who disappear into their cells of technology – mobile phones, the Internet, video games. They withdraw into an obsessiveness not unlike the syndrome pop psychologists in the United States have called "Internet addiction," in which complete absorption in an artificial world is preferable to any encounters in the real one.

Government statistics report that 120,000 students dropped out of high school in 1999, a twenty percent increase from two years earlier. Incidents of student violence toward teachers rose eleven percent in 1999, reaching a record 36,600 cases perpetrated by elementary, junior-high and high-school students. High-profile criminal cases in the summer of 2000, such as the bus hijacking by a seventeen-year-old who fatally wounded an elderly woman, and another in which a seventeen-year-old beat his mother to death, inspired legislation that lowered the age at which criminal defendants may be prosecuted as adults. Japan's National Police Agency estimates that the number of juveniles held for serious crimes – including robbery and murder – rose by fifty-one percent between 1997 and 1998 alone.

Japanese newspapers run stories of laid-off businessmen donning their suits each morning and dashing out of the house to spend their days reading through classifieds in local cafes or libraries, determined to hide their joblessness from wives and children. Men comprise seventy-one percent of national suicide totals. In a kind of crypto-Victorian nightmare, Japan's recession is killing those most invested in trying to conceal its effects.

As Japanese parents cling desperately to an old and collapsing order, the kids are trying to let go, to find and define life's values without prescribed schemes – and they are finding it difficult.

It was in Japan, unexpectedly, that I began to recognize a dissonance that I felt intimately. The powerful need to belong to something larger than oneself permeates Japanese life. The knowing gestures and refined graces of women of my grandmother's generation, like performing a tea ceremony for visitors in the afternoon, resonate with the perfectly replicated hairstyles and makeup of elaborately outfitted teenagers hitting the streets of Shibuya for an all-night club crawl. Young Japanese finally seem frustrated at having to comply, yet afraid of the elemental loneliness that is the punishment for straying too far on one's own.

The second time I met with Haruki Murakami, he was more forthcoming about the generation with which he occasionally communicates via his website.

"Many of them ask me questions about love," he said, smiling wistfully, then turning somber. "Many young people want to be loved for being themselves, and they don't know how. They don't understand. I think younger people in Japan are beginning to understand the virtues of independence, but it's not easy to be independent. It's very lonely, actually. It's very hard to be an individual."

Even as Japan instills conformity in its citizens, the nation has always tried to set itself apart – through strategic military and industrial isolation, through language, custom and idiosyncrasy. Since the first incursion of American Admiral Matthew Perry's so-called black ships in 1853 and the subsequent Meiji Restoration in the latter half of the nineteenth century, the Japanese have worked toward achieving economic parity with the West while distinguishing themselves from their Asian neighbors. Right-wing zealots still argue that Japan's colonial aggression before World War II was singularly heroic, a way of "saving" weaker Eastern countries from Western imperialists, however disastrous the global consequences.

Now the pressure is on Japan once again – to conform and to be unique. In the current American-led conflicts in the Middle East, Japan is being asked to serve as the loyal ally – an unquestioning, ever-faithful samurai, a dedicated salaryman – by sending troops into battles instigated by their former conquerors. But Prime Minister Junichiro Koizumi's televised calls for Japan to act "responsibly" in seeking "global stability" fall on deaf ears, at least among the young people I've spoken to. "We feel sorry for America," one Shibuya teenager told me recently. "But we don't need your wars because we're Japan. You're America. Your problems are not our problems."

A few months before I returned to New York, I visited Hiroshima and its Peace Museum, an imposing concrete edifice only a short walk from the skeletal Hiroshima dome, which was the only structure left standing in the wake of the bomb's sudden, indiscriminate fury. Among the horrific inventory of artifacts from the blast, I kept returning to a boy's junior-high-school uniform, its edges curled incongruously. The intense heat burst the boy's body, so the buttonholes were blasted outward; the fabric is frayed into sharp points that reach toward you through the glass encasement.

More than half a century after the bombing of Hiroshima, many of my former students wore uniforms just like this one to school each day, the high collars and lean jackets suggesting dignity, self-control, discipline and social unity. But aren't they also a form of protection, a way of warding off ridicule by ensuring that the individual would not visibly stand out, or stand alone? *Kireru* is another new Japanese word, denoting the perpetration of a sudden, violent act, when an individual has snapped, having reached a breaking point. Like those buttonholes blown spastically outward, the word *kireru* connotes the inner self losing control and bursting into irrational rage. The term is applied to the young when they attack bystanders or family members for no apparent reason, when violence erupts from within and cannot be contained. Social critics blame everything from Western-style junk food to violent comic books and video games, but Terasawa offers another take: "Modern society is all surfaces. It is amazing and powerful. And it's so simple. But here and here" – he touches his chest, then his head – "there is nothing at all."

KŪHAKU

david cady
illustrations by kozyndan

kūhaku [kuuhaku] 空白 *n.*

1. A blank; blank [empty] space. *Tabula rasa.*
2. A vacuum, a void. A power vacuum. A blank in one's memory. [Kūhaku no mikkakan] *Went missing for three days.* Interregnum.

a. [Kūhaku o sonjuru] Leave [produce] a vacuum; make a blank [in one's life]. [Kūhaku o mitasu] Fill a gap in; fill up a blank. [Kūhaku o iu] To utter a codeword; an attempt to give meaning where none is apparent. *He uttered* "kūhaku" *as if to fill a void and watched as his cup overflowed.*
b. [Kūhaku ga] Leave a blank. [Ooki na kūhaku ga dekita] Leave a great blank. *His sense of loss left a great blank in his life.*

kūbaku [kuubaku] 空白

1. blank; blank [empty] space; [blank area].
1. A vacuum; a void. A power vacuum. A blank in one's memory. [Kūbaku no tsukiōkan. What missing for those days] Interregnum.

a. Kūbaku o umidasu | Leave [produce] a vacuum; make a blank [in one's life]. Kūbaku o mitasu | Fill a gap in; fill up a blank. Kūbaku o tsuku | To utter a code word; an attempt to give meaning where none is apparent. He uttered "kūbaku," as if to fill a void and watched as his cup overflowed.

b. Kūbaku ga | Leave a blank. [Ooki na] Kūbaku ga deshita | Leave a great blank. The sense of loss left a great blank in his life.

Shimotakaido Station

McDonald's
Bargain Kaijo (flea market)
Mikasa-ya (Japanese sweets)
Tanaka-sanchi no Kutsuyasan (The Tanaka's Shoe Store) (shoe store)
Origin Bento (box lunches/deli)
Kasaoki Soba (1F)
Kudo Juhan (1F, real estate agency)
Gakusei Loan (2F, student loan office)
Haikara ConCon Honpo (2F, restaurant)
Boutique Queen (women's clothing)
Shimotakaido Dream House (lottery ticket vendor)
Ivy (1F, glasses/contacts shop)
Hairshop Ziggy (2F)
Keibi Design Service (3F, security service shop)
Hirata Chiropractor (4F, chiropractor)
Keitai Denwa Chiiki Ichiban Ten (cellphone shop)
Ootova (B1, Japanese-style restaurant)
Hamatora (1F, *okonomiyaki, monja*)
Karaoke (2F)
Sengoku (3F, spaghetti, tempura restaurant)
Yamada-ya (1F, bug shop)
Kent House (2F, rental info shop)

La Mieux (beauty salon)
Pallette Plaza Digital Pallette (film developer)
Oniwa Kami Bungu Ten (stationery shop)
Shiratori Koshiji (tempura, hot pot restaurant)
Matsumoto Kiyoshi (drugstore)
Discshop Oscar (CD/tape/video sales)
Relax Refresh Center (2F, shiatsu massage shop)
Nagao Kesshohinya (1F, makeup shop)
Kohikan (2F, coffee shop)
Curry House CoCo Ichibanya (1F, Japanese-style curry restaurant)
Jitensha Shimada (bike store/repair)
Salon de Tea Cagny (tea/cake shop)
Boutique Queen (women's fashion)

Oturo (2F, Japanese bar)
Anshin-do Shoten (1F, bookstore)
Sara Sara (2F, Italian restaurant)

Akamatsu Koban (police box)

7-Eleven (convenience store)

Matsuzawa Elementary School

Co Raku (Chinese restaurant)
Yama-ni Fudosan (real estate agency)
Kusuri Seijo (drugstore)
Torigin (yakitori)
Iwata (barbershop)
Bunka-do Shoten (magazine/bookstore)
Can Do 100 Yen Shop (100 yen shop)
Waseda Academy (2F, cram school)
Watami (2F, Japanese-style bar/restaurant)
T-Comp (1F, CD/video rental/record shop)
Saeki (basement, grocery store)
Jonathan (family restaurant)
Gyu-Kyaku (2F, braised beef restaurant)
Matsuya (1F, Japanese beef bowl restaurant)
Il-Pissaro (women's clothing)
Baserinton (3F, language/math studies school)
Kazu Dental Clinic (2F)
Tendon Tenya (1F, tempura restaurant)
Amataro (2F, Japanese-style bar)
shalala Bird (1F, knick-knack shop)
Ftm (1F, beauty salon)
Game You You (B1, video game arcade)
UFJ Bank ATM
Matsunaga Tailors (tailor)
Soba Nami (noodle restaurant)
Tawamiya (sweet bean cake shop)
Tatsumi (beer/dining tavern)

Sushi-tsune (sushi shop)
Chinese qigong clinic (3F)
Tanning Resort (2F, tanning salon)
Topboy (1F, video game software, sales)
Harry's (Basement, bar)
Mesaki Chiryoshitsu (chiropractor, osteopathy)
Fukushi Kissa YOU you (cake, tea, coffee shop)
Matsuzawa City Office (town hall)
eSol (2F, tanning-bed sales office)
Internet Space Planet (1F, Internet café)
Hanyu Clinic (1F, medical clinic)
Branch (dry cleaner)
Musashiya (rice shop)
Sankei Shimbun delivery base
Hair Savor (beauty salon)
Koyama Liquor Store
Nenkumi (cellphone retail shop)
Antenna (2F, hair salon)
Pearl Dental Clinic (2F)
Shinobe Clinic (1F, internal medicine clinic)
Vitamin produced by Crossroads International (women's clothing)
Steps (bar)
In Control (women's clothing)
Bon Vivant (flower shop)
Long Hair (used clothing)

Painthouse Carestation 21 (home reform service shop)
Seikodo (jewelry shop)
Aurore (bakery)
Ryo-an (tea/Japanese traditional gift shop)
Right On (jeans, casual clothing)
House Shimotakaido (apt. building)
Photo Iwaki (photo developer)
Kodama Futon Ten (futon/bedding shop)
Volunteer fire station
Apartment building
Iida Tofu-ten (tofu shop)
Great Indian (Indian curry)
Sam (used CDs, records, laser discs)
Shion (beauty salon)
Kutsu no Chitose (shoe store)
Panache (basement, Western food restaurant)

Nyan-ya (antique store)

Futon no Futabaya (futon/bedding shop)

Takahashi Construction Works (office)

Hair Salon Yamaguchi

boarded-up shop

auto garage warehouse

apartment building

Cleaning Kojima (dry cleaner)

Znet (2F, cram school/computer school)

Mambo (1F, men's clothing)
Hair Shop Ziggy2 (beauty salon)
Lifecare Akazutsumi (reflexology)
Bombay Juice (funky knick-knacks, incense)

Luce (1F, Italian restaurant)
Disc Gallery (2F, buy/sell CDs, records)

Okumara Acupuncture, Moxibustion and Chiropractic Clinic

Uoshige (seafood shop)

Swallows Chain (1F, dry cleaner)

Nichidatsu Dental Clinic (2F)

Chinese astrology shop

Apartment building

Chushin-Ken Shokudo (Japanese restaurant)

Maruhide (ramen shop)

Fujiya (Japanese restaurant)

Mammy (corner store)

here are no
eighteen-
hundred-year-old

pine trees lining this *g o d d a m n* street,
which is seven strides wide and

has no sidewalks, but there is a
cherry tree, and it **blooms**

every spring in front of the elementary
school over a faded
                and
       creepy mural

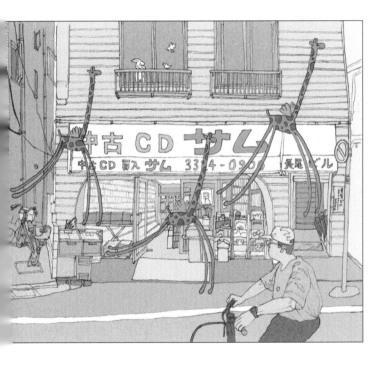

painted by skinny, *hyper* students about fifteen years ago.

You could say this street is like a river
– a ^riv_{er} of ^{li}fe[1] – but let's just say that
it gets *pretty* crowded sometimes,

[1] *Please clap on each syllable of this phrase.*

and if you're not ca_reful,
some high school girl

will *ring* *ring* *ring* her bicycle bell at you and *harpoon* ~~you~~ with a **reproachful glance** as she whooshes by,

an act that will stick in your craw

BIG-TIME,

because you did nothing wrong, seeing as
there
was
no
sidewalk
to seek refuge on.

GARBAGE
sharon moshavi

N O ONE LIKES taking out the garbage. But in Japan the chore is compounded by an added element: the neighbors are watching. No, I'm not being paranoid. They're watching. Every time I take my trash down to the curb, in its regulation translucent white bag, I can feel their eyes peering through the plastic at my milk cartons, my egg containers, my disposable chopsticks. They can see everything.

I first realized my garbage and I were not alone on a Monday a few months ago, when I was bringing down a bag of old cereal boxes, soggy refrigerator leftovers and coffee grounds. My landlady, who lives on the first floor, was outside watering her garden. Her eyes took in the contents of my trash.

"No, today is Monday. It's plastics day," she said.

"Oh," I replied, "I guess they changed the pickup schedule."

Her eyes fluttered to the ground, studiously avoiding mine. No, Monday has always been plastics day, she said.

Over the next few minutes, in the muddled mix of Japanese and English we use to communicate, my landlady explained that she often would take my garbage away if I had put it out on the wrong day, store it in her house and then bring it out again on the proper day.

As I walked back upstairs, lugging my unwanted trash, it hit me: for the year and a half since I'd been living in the apartment, she'd been watching me. Peeping from behind her rose bushes. Scurrying to the curb after I'd been there, checking to see whether I'd followed the correct garbage protocol.

That's when I learned the hard truth: when it comes to garbage in Japan, there's no such thing as privacy. Garbage is public property, something to which your neighbors can claim snooping privileges. As a foreigner in this homogenous land, my activities garner more attention, and more criticism, than most. I've started wondering what else my neighbors notice. Which of my habits or my comings and goings are fodder for them? What else am I doing wrong?

What I found most disturbing about the exchange was that my landlady had been reluctant for so long to confront me directly. We see each other constantly. Sometimes we have pleasant little chats, or she comes upstairs when something is broken, and yet she could never bear to tell me that I had mixed up the trash schedule. Pointing out one's mistakes is considered rude in Japan.

As a foreigner with rudimentary Japanese, I expected the language barrier to be the biggest obstacle in living here. I was wrong. Learning to navigate Japan, perhaps any foreign country, is all about reading the subtle cultural cues, not the alphabet. Most things in Japan remain unspoken, especially the improper and the unpleasant.

The unsaid, though, does not remain untouched. My garbage has been invaded once again. Now another neighbor, an elderly man, has taken to donning latex surgical gloves and combing through the piles of garbage on the street, bag by bag. The thought that a piece of plastic might have slipped in on a day for paper or, heaven forbid, a piece of paper on plastics day, is just too much for him to bear. Sometimes, I spy on him myself, watching through the curtains to see whether my bag of garbage has passed muster. I wait fearfully for the day he knocks on my door, an outstretched, accusing hand holding one of my soda cans, which had inadvertently been mixed in with the plastic bottles.

That day probably will never come. My mistake will not be pointed out to me directly. It will be carried on the wings of neighborhood gossip, the tale of the foreign lady who cannot properly sort her trash.

Living abroad, I've had my privacy invaded in all sorts of ways. In Japan, the invasion feels like a stealth attack; in India, where I once lived, it's more of a direct assault. There, everyone was quick to comment on nearly everything I did. Not just my actions, but my home itself was fair game. In Japan, the home remains off-limits to outsiders; in New Delhi, the outside charges in, delivering, fixing, cleaning – and snooping. Your life is not your own.

Neither is your garbage. Just throw it out the window, and trash becomes someone else's problem. You never have to think about it again. The result: mounds of trash clutter the streets and foul the air.

The Japanese, with their fixation on cleanliness, have gone perhaps too far to the other extreme. Now, don't get me wrong. I'm all for recycling. Separating, as the Japanese do, between organic waste, plastics, cans and other recyclables is commendable. But the vigilance with which Japanese make sure the trash rules are followed has little to do with environmental awareness. I think it has everything to do with a Japanese love of the system, *any* system. Garbage, like much else in Japan, is about following the rules and making sure everyone else does too. It's about keeping an eye on each other, but pretending not to.

If the Japanese really wanted to be environmentally responsible, they'd stop burning all their plastic garbage. They'd stop suffocating every purchase in countless layers of wrapping. I mean, does each apple really need to be individually encased in plastic and Styrofoam? Do I need to rip open paper, plastic, cardboard, then plastic again to get to a bar of soap?

Sometimes I feel like I'm drowning in trash. I've literally had to turn my second bathroom into a garbage storage room. Some items, which don't seem to fit into any garbage category, have sat there for months. But even when the trash is piled up to the ceiling, part of me would rather just leave it there. I can't bear the thought of making that trip down the stairs and across the street, knowing that my Japanese neighbors' eyes are on me. Watching.

ANSWERS TO CORRESPONDENTS

cal ranson

S OMEONE ONCE SAID that in order to know a community, one must know its funerals. 'Mrs. Jones' in Kyushu, if you really wish to know how to conduct yourself during native rites, I can enlighten you.

The first hardship you will be forced to endure for the sake of the dear departed is a wake, known as *otsuya*, at which time you'll be forced to consume endless gallons of the most vile-tasting beer. Naturally, it would be disrespectful to decline, so make the most of it.

If you're at all serious about the departed soul, especially if you loathed him, light an incense stick in front of the coffin, wave it around until all concerned have witnessed the depths of your sorrow and plant it upright in the provided mound of ash. If you've ever wondered why not to do the same with your chopsticks in a bowl of rice, you now know.

When the fat priest arrives by scooter at his appointed time, feel free to ignore him and any ritual he performs near the body – he's only in it for the money. This may be an appropriate juncture to check your dress. Black and white only – red is far too jolly and may clash with the rouge on the corpse's cheeks.

The *ososhiki*, AKA the funeral itself, usually takes place the next day, so bring your wallet. The cover charge at a Japanese funeral is generally somewhere between outrageous and financially crippling – you may prefer a place inside the casket next time – and collected only in the crispest of banknotes within the regulation envelope. A profit for the grieving widow is not unexpected. If you are a pauper, don't worry; your time will surely come.

Typically, unless a satanic service is in order, our rotund cleric flops his wobbling jowls round the door again to justify his standing in the community, possibly offering a sutra or two to distract heathens from the concrete and plastic beauty of the funeral hall. Skipping the reading of mailed-in condolences from those too busy washing their hair to attend the highlight of their former friend's existence, proceed directly to the viewing of the body and thence the cremation.

Whether through lack of space or some other equally preposterous Japanese myth, ashes to ashes is the rule. A decent fellow takes an hour and a half to be well done, a scoundrel considerably longer on account of the weight of his sins. Either way, the result is the same – a pile of ash and bones on a tray for the family to pick over.

Unless you're kin, you may be excused the gruesome ritual of passing shards of bone by chopstick to your neighbor and on into an urn, whence a pestle is employed to grind the last remnants of life out of your ex-associate. Critical at this juncture is to pick out the succulent Adam's apple and save it for a rainy day – you never know when it might come in handy.

¶ 'Mostly Honest John':

I respect your assertion that twenty-seven and a third relatively trouble-free years in Takamatsuhamaoka-mura without learning more than a thimbleful of Japanese is proof positive that English is indeed a prince amongst languages, but I can't help but worry that your dear wife must be terribly put upon.

You say she's an asset in so many areas of your life, that you need utter nary a *konnichiwa* for yourself, which is undeniably a good thing; however, where does that place you in the community's eyes? Far be it for this humble scribe to suggest that you could be doing yourself a disservice by hiding behind the skirts of your native mate, although I will put forward the opinion that not all view your position with such understanding.

Doubtless, closed doors and mute walls have been witness in your absence to many a verbal attack upon your integrity. Have you heard nothing of this when going about your daily business? Of course, epithets like *gaijin* and *bakayaro* are surely water off your broad back these days, but do the inevitable comparisons between the humungous proportions of your nose and its inverse correlation to your "husbandliness" not trouble you? I have heard of men in your situation losing all will to live – you would do well to bear that in mind.

I know your village well. It is one of the finer hamlets untouched by either swine fever or doomsday cults. Your situation suggests that you could yet have failed to penetrate the inner circle that is so important to country folk. If you wish to ease the burden on your wife while maintaining the façade that you too are an educated creature, you might try smiling broadly and nodding slowly when asked a question in Japanese. Should the question concern the weather, the state of the nation or should it even be an inquiry as to how your nasty rash is faring, a substantial display of teeth and an incline of the head will lubricate proceedings considerably. When told you are truly a kind man for looking after your wife so, please take it as the insult it is intended to be and thank your benefactor with an "*arigato gozaimasu*" as you remove yourself swiftly from the scene.

On no account attempt to respond with anything wordier than a brace of words strung together like plump grouse. A more substantial grapple with the language will win you the compliment, "*Nihongo jozu desu ne*," and we wouldn't want that, would we?

❡ 'Mrs. A':
    I wholeheartedly agree with your desire to rein your husband in a touch. Next time he heads off to Bangkok for a spot of "how's your father," tell him to pack his own prophylactics.

❡ 'Concerned Visitor':
    Yes, when I first made town, it was rather a surprise to

discover there are real, live homeless people in a city so clinical as Tokyo. You claim a desire to help, but lack the knowledge of where to start. Allow me.

I propose you sit yourself down and address a letter to the governor, one of whose predecessors, a Mr. Aoshima, believed: "Those homeless people have a unique philosophy. They like to live like that."

Shocking indeed, but surely your voice will be heard above the mute masses. You may want to offer the governor a guided evening tour of Shinjuku station. The sight of row upon row of ragged men should give him pause for thought, or at least remind him that his city is "home" to over ten thousand such folk.

As you rightly point out, most of these people are not what Western eyes might expect – young runaways, drinkers, drugtakers or crackpots; they are middle-aged men who have fallen victim to the most prolonged recession in modern Japan.

Take Mr. Tanaka, an acquaintance of mine renowned in his circle for securing the day's used newspapers to resell almost before their ink is dry. But a year ago, aged fifty-three, Tanaka found himself out of a job when his employer shut up shop after some rumpus over unpaid taxes. A lifetime of supporting three children meant funds were already low and, when his thankless wife filed for divorce (the shame of a jobless husband!) and moved in with her sister, Tanaka was left with a house he couldn't pay for and twelve years to wait before welfare was available to him.

Being a proud man and unwilling to ask those members of his family who could bear to speak to him for aid, he had little option but to take up residence in West Shinjuku's cardboard city. Now, I have nothing against these paper dwellings – the murals on some would shame Michelangelo and their cleanliness disgrace an operating room – but the attitude of the public was a bitter pill.

Violent attacks by teenagers who view the homeless as

mere sport are the stock in trade of the evening news. Why, I don't know. Could it be something to do with the opinion-shaping powers of those at the top of the tree? Could it be that these children have such low self-esteem, they seek out others seemingly in a worse position? It's impossible to know for sure, but asking the question of the folk in charge could be a start.

It's not all grim down Shinjuku way, my man Tanaka tells me:

"I suppose being homeless has its good points – I don't have to listen to my wife's infernal racket, there's plenty of room for my shoes in the *genkan*, and I can have my box just the way I like it. But if one more department store security guard makes that godforsaken crossed forearms gesture to bar my passage, I'll swing for him."

¶ 'Disgruntled English Teacher':

No sir, you are not obliged to remain awake for the entirety of a lesson. Your students are even less likely to raise a fuss than they are to comment on the hideous necktie and half-mast "white boy special" trousers I'm quite sure you take pride in wearing. On that note, you may want to consider a trip to an apparel store somewhat closer to home – I find it works wonders for a spirit weary of twenty-five-inch inseams.

¶ 'Young Mother':

Whilst I appreciate the fact that your little emperor is undoubtedly a work of the finest art, I find it hard to condone his sleeping in the marital futon at the expense of his father. All right-thinking folk must surely be aware that an eight-year-old boy is no substitute for a spouse, no matter how whiskey soaked either of the pair might be.

Try as you might to raise the lad respectably – and reading between your lines, I sense a certain over-eager, not to mention illegal, effort to squeeze the child into your husband's shoes – your spawn must be left to his own devices and not mollycoddled to within an inch of his life. Continuing down this path leads only to moral bankruptcy and one more twig on the tinder pile of dysfunctional youth. Leave him be.

¶ 'Eyes Down,' Harajuku:

Your dilemma encapsulates the eternal inner struggle of any foreign resident of this near-homogenous nation. When out for your evening constitutional, do you stick to your policy of refusing to see other non-Japanese as if they were made of air, or do you slap the back and wring the hand of every big-nosed passerby? (We'll leave the Asian neighbors out of this for now, as I see no way to extend my sweeping generalizations their length.)

Generally, those fresh off the boat tend to prefer the friendlier course of action, such is their shock at finding themselves in an alien environment. Seeking comfort from strangers is understandable when surrounded by such uncivilized beasts as the Japanese. If you do choose to follow this path, there is a right way and a wrong way, of course.

Incorrect: Making a body's acquaintance in a polite, considered manner – asking the time of day or if you can receive directions to the station are red-hot ways to win an enemy. Be sure to eschew such old hat.

Correct: Approach your target from the front with a firm jaw and an outstretched paw. Take his hand and squeeze like he was your long-lost brother, returned from the front. Drag him into a tavern and proceed immediately to over-familiarity.

Compulsory conversational topics include (preferably in this order), how much you despise: your job, the Japanese, the food, the weather, the Japanese, your excessively compliant girlfriend, the Japanese and, finally, your tiny apartment.

You can then move on to how long each of you has been

in country, what exactly it is you do and the likelihood of your staying long-term, but on no account ask your jawing partner's name. Opinion is divided as to the acceptability of rubbing your hands with glee and yamming about how you love the heaps of yen stuffed under your mattress – any positivity is often frowned upon.

You may quiz your newest best friend about the possibility of exchanging those bothersome girlfriends or whether he'd care for a trip to that lady of the night you know who can make your cares melt away for a few thousand yen (early birds only – a little more after noon). Lastly, don't overlook the mandate to abuse the locals that comes free with your sixth beer.

❡ 'Gordon Blue':
It is fine to adulterate your bowl of white rice with catsup if it's a spell in the city jail you're after. As for your suggestion that the sashimi would go down easier with a good roasting and some butter sauce, good luck to you – you'll need it.

❡ 'Jonah':
You raise a fine point, and I think I agree with your desire to see a touch less wrapping on your purchases. It's one thing to receive a hot dog wreathed in plastic upon plastic, but your account of a gift-wrapped sausage dog is too much.

❡ 'Dirk X' writes from Roppongi, eager to share his good fortune and success with the local ladies. He notes:

> "Even on a quiet night, I still manage to score – at least once. I highly recommend the single life in Japan to anyone at a loose end or seeking a loose woman."

Sir, not that I'm an expert in these matters, but could it be something other than your sheer charisma and fine odor that makes you such a dynamo? In fact, there's a nasty rumor doing the rounds to the effect that your white face and blue eyes are effective antidotes to your vile persona.

Moreover, I'm told the lingering impression of the pox upon your face and your diminished stature are no deterrent to these fine young women, who gaze upon even the humblest of Westerners with goo-goo eyes. You say you're an investment banker; ordinarily, that would be reason enough to shun your company, but could it be that the only tumescence your companions desire is in your pocketbook?

Does your wooden leg not hamper proceedings? Perhaps the glass eye gives a misleading impression from time to time? I heard your inability to go more than six or seven minutes without an alcoholic beverage makes you wonderful company, so that may weigh in your favor, I suppose.

Carry on – I wish you the best of luck in not contracting a condition worse than your rancid character.

¶ 'Woe is Them' wishes to know what it is she can do to improve the lot of the "poor, uncreative" Japanese salaryman. Madam, all I can offer you is an exhortation not to get too close to the bars and, most especially, not to feed the animals.

You may think your three years within the hive and ability to eat *natto* qualify you to know better than an entire nation – and I'm not about to quibble with you – but I hear it is something of a challenge to teach an old mutt new tricks. Take the habit of the common barcode-crested salaryman to shuffle papers around his desk till midnight with the sole aim of passing time until the boss takes his leave. I doubt your cries of "get a life" will make a great deal of difference anytime before the Styx freezes over.

Better to help him back to the land of the living with a

few tricks designed to avoid him shooting his bolt too early in the day. Sabotage his company-mandated *rajio taiso* early-morning aerobics class with a sneaky call for assistance at a fictitious filing "situation," thereby helping conserve what little energy he may have. Admittedly, he may be unable to resist the convention of running to the emergency with all the grace of a baby elephant, but being seen to do his bit will elevate his intra-office standing, at least until a colleague can trump him, perhaps with an unbroken seventy-two-hour stint at his post or by donating a kidney to the company president.

¶ 'Matsuo Jr,' Iga Ueno:
   Your efforts at making a Haiku-ist of yourself can be considered bearable, but only just. I reproduce them here as a caution to our readers:

> *Old pond …*
> *a frog leaps in*
> *water's sound.*

   Seeing your words in print just now, I trust you realize where you've gone wrong – your verse just doesn't scan, old bean. Of course, that kind of slackness may pass muster before the filthy masses in Iga Ueno, but it just won't do in the more erudite locales. It entertains as much as a geometry workbook and soothes no more than stinging nettles. Take yourself back to the drawing board with a large glass of whiskey and a sleeping pill.
   PS It doesn't rhyme either.

¶ 'Roger':
   Feel free to get in the *onsen* wearing a coat of soap suds. It's only mineral-rich hot spring water, and there's plenty more where that came from. You dolt.

THAT FLOATING FEELING II
sumie kawakami
translation by yuko enomoto

Naomi Kawai is a twenty-nine-year-old actress. She was
interviewed in April 2003.

WHILE PREPARING TO MOVE, I found a beige-colored beret in the corner of the closet. As I took it in my hand, the sting of mothballs made me feel a little light-headed.

My husband bought me that hat shortly after we met. It was similar to the one Bonnie wears in *Bonnie and Clyde*, the movie we saw after a few dates. Bonnie and Clyde were real criminals in America. And, in the movie, the couple falls deeper and deeper in love as they go on a criminal rampage that finally pushes them over the edge.

"Bonnie is just like you: simple and innocent, yet temperamental," my future husband said. In reality, I did not like Faye Dunaway's shallow portrayal of Bonnie, so I am sure I looked unhappy. My husband must have found my displeasure amusing because we walked into a department store that was right next to the theater, and he asked the store clerk, "Do you have a beige beret?" Then he placed the beret on my head and kissed me on the cheek. He didn't care that people may have been watching.

There is a saying that goes something like, "There is beauty in love because it is built on sin." Whether or not that is true, I believe that husbands and wives are partners in crime. The relationship between a husband and a wife is ideally a positive one based on a shared past and a unique culture built through years of living together. But then, one day, one small thing goes wrong, and everything from then on falls slightly out of kilter. They go on with their lives as usual, but one day they realize that they have strayed from the norm and have entered into a special world, a dark abyss far removed from social standards and common sense. It seems that the more you try to climb out of it, the deeper you will fall. The truth is, neither one of you has any intention to return to the life you once knew, and the abyss itself becomes the norm.

Husbands and wives at the terminal stage of a deteriorating marriage are straitjacketed by their own selfish ways, aren't they? One of them is thinking, "If we stay together, we will destroy each other. But I can't be on my own yet. I am scared. I do not know how to live on my own." And so, without making any progress, the couple stays in that state of mutual hurt. That scent of danger is what constitutes complicity, I think.

I did not cheat on my husband to hurt him. And in the end, that's not why we got divorced. I was just very lonely. I realized it immediately after we got married: my husband will never be able to fill the void in my heart. That realization made me feel very lonely. My state of mind at the time was, "Maybe I should sell my body." We got married because we were in love, but soon afterward, it all came crashing down on us.

I am the type of person who tries to make things happen – whether at work or romance. My husband, on the other hand, tends to leave things up to fate, as if he is waiting for something to come his way. When we got married, he asked me, "Do you want to be happy?" Not, "I will make you happy."

Looking back, I did have some misgivings about a future with a man like him. As a student, I liked plays, and I aspired to become an actress. My husband was a novice producer and had just released his first work. I met my husband through a friend from the theater company I worked for at the time. The friend invited me to the opening night of my future husband's production.

It was a safe production. There were no structural errors that would've been the death knell of this play. It had the right amount of originality in technique, actors with just enough character and smart twists to the whole piece, whether or not they were intended to woo the media. But I instinctively knew this was just a work of ego. Here and there, the piece just turned in on itself, leaving the audience in the dark. It was oozing with such fierce indifference, it seemed to say, "I do not care about the audience." His disregard for others was chilling.

After the curtains closed, I wrote on a questionnaire: "This is just a work of ego." My friend introduced me to him, but this being his first production, he was extremely busy. The play left a bitter taste in my mouth, so after we exchanged greetings, I made a quick exit.

If we had never met again, we would have lived completely separate lives. Were our paths destined to cross? A year later, he came to see our play. We hardly spoke to each other. It was like meeting him for the first time. Also, he had read my comments, so he knew I didn't like his work.

After the play, he initiated the conversation. This, in effect, was how we started going out.

In the beginning, our relationship was based on a shared interest – the theater. My husband was already past thirty, and – presumably, not wanting to miss the opportunity to get married – he proposed to me only three months after we started dating. Still a student at the time, I vaguely thought, "Maybe marriage isn't the right thing." But as graduation neared, I wavered. I enjoyed studying so I considered going into graduate studies. I also wanted to pursue theater work. But I was not confident about making a living that way. At the same time, I felt the need to solidify my plans for the future. Not only had I spent extra time studying after finishing high school, I also stayed on two extra years in college, busy with the theater (although at the time, staying on was considered something of a status symbol). I knew I couldn't waste any more time. But the more I thought about it, the less I knew what to do.

On the one hand, I was eager to leave my parents and start my own family. I am an only child, and I know I was brought up in a loving environment. But because my mother was such an unstable person, I felt oppressed by the dark atmosphere of our home. I grew up thinking that that was normal, until I started visiting friends' houses and saw the father sauntering around in his underwear. Then, I knew some homes

were warmer than ours, and that made me feel a little sad. For
my father, work was always secondary to my mother's well being. I used to watch my father and think, "He has thrown away
his life for mother." As a social being, I could not respect such
a father. My admiration of older men may have stemmed from
my yearning for the ideal father figure.

Come to think of it, my husband is not the typical dependable type. First of all, his income is unstable, which is not
unusual for this industry. He is long on social skills and very
good with people, yet he is emotionally frail. Even then, I knew
I wanted to support him.

Looking back, that was a masculine decision on my part.
I was just a student. I hadn't made my societal debut at that
point, and there I was deciding to help support a man. At the
time, it seemed like a wonderful thing to do. I believed that together we could achieve anything, whereas alone, he would fail.
We shared a common dream: the theater. My husband's work
was not perfect by any means. I guess that's why I wanted to
support him.

Ironic, is it not? I always saw my father as the coward
who squelched his life for the family (at least, that's the way it
seemed to me at the time). But, as a result, I practically went
out of my way to do the same thing.

We got married in the winter I turned twenty-five, just
a few months shy of graduation in February. My husband was
twelve years older, and some voiced objections that I was too
young to get married. The strange thing was, the more people
objected, the more I felt it was the right thing to do.

My husband was from a wealthy family and was getting
financial assistance from them when we got married. Well, I
didn't like that. So, as soon as we got married, I got a job at a
small firm and asked him to decline their help.

The setbacks came as soon as we got married. Our sex
life ended with marriage. Sex was great when we were still
lovers. "My relationships with women usually end in eight

months," my husband once said, "but I've lasted a year with you. I think we can make it." Later, he would say it wasn't working out. I lost confidence in myself. I thought I was no longer attractive.

Strange thing, though. Once you lose confidence, your conviction to win someone over becomes stronger. After a while, I started to make the first move. In the beginning, my husband would reluctantly comply. But eventually, he began to call my actions "dirty." The rejection was so blunt that I put the blame on myself: I was too loose. That made me feel even more wretched. In my daily life with my husband, I was constantly being desexualized.

Perhaps he is a misogynist? Come to think of it, he once told me that as a young student he used to put his hands over his ears during sex education because he couldn't stand even listening to such discussions. "Sex is for procreation," he would say, revealing his philosophy that any woman who wanted sex was dirty. For example, when doing the laundry, he would wash everything but my underwear, which he would leave at the bottom of the washing machine, saying something like, "I do not like such things." I felt completely denied. Is my existence so filthy? Just the thought of the contempt he had for me as a woman battered my confidence. I do not understand to this day why he rejected sex in such a manner.

I tried to understand that he had his own ideal female figure. Lest I destroy that, I stopped initiating sex. I told myself that in areas other than sex I felt his affection for me, and, that was good enough. In fact, he was a very kind person when he was in a good mood. As far as my acting was concerned, he would say, "You are still young. I don't want to destroy your potential." One time when I woke up, without any warning, he scooped me out of bed, as if I were a princess. "I wanted to make sure I can lift you up in case of an earthquake," he said. I remember feeling so happy then – to the point of tears.

The irony is, in *Bonnie and Clyde*, Clyde, who is not gay,

keeps spurning Bonnie's advances, saying he does not like women. But in the movie, the two end up together. That's why, somewhere in the corner of my heart, I felt that we were going to be alright.

But sex was not the only problem. He had convinced my parents that he would work very hard, even do manual labor, to win the hand of their daughter. And yet, as soon as we rented a place and moved in together, he started spending the days at home. In the beginning, I earned more money, so he helped me with the housework. But when I came home tired from work, he appeared to be so free with his time. I used to think, "There are plenty of things I would love to do but can't." I felt bitter. I am sure jealousy played a part. My husband was already working in theater, and I hadn't even taken a first step in that direction. But, watching my husband's easygoing ways made me think, "Well, I am going to have a life of leisure, too." And so, only several months after I landed a new job, I resigned.

There were days back then when both of us were at home in the afternoon. I used to get so angry just thinking about how we were getting old as we sat out in the sun, passing the time away. The world of the theater was quickly slipping away from my grasp while I was being straitjacketed by our mundane daily life.

I still remember one afternoon, when we went grocery shopping. The summer sun was beating down on the vegetables, and as soon as I saw that, I felt a sudden chill. "What on earth am I doing?" I thought to myself. At the same time, I felt an anger welling up inside and came so close to tossing an entire basket full of onions at my husband.

Of course, I still had some sense left in me. "I'm leaving," I said, and as I turned to go, my husband just cast a suspicious glance at me.

The first time I had a relationship with anybody other than my husband was about six months after we got married.

At the time I didn't realize it, but there was a feminine side to me. I strangely identified with the passage in a novel I was reading at the time that said, "I don't want to sleep alone tonight, so I will pick up a man in the park." That's how lonely I felt. "Should I sell my body?" I thought. Of course, I didn't go that far.

That day, my husband was on a business trip, so I went out drinking with an old friend from college. He always held me in high regard and used to say to me, "You could go far in the academic world. What a waste to get married." Having opposed my getting married, he had been concerned about how I was getting along. When he heard that I wasn't doing too well, he gave me the old, "I told you so. I knew it wasn't for you."

I have always been a word person. I love verbal exchanges, debates and talking things through. But my husband doesn't. Perhaps he felt that talking was useless; he used to go silent on me whenever we had an argument. That drove me crazy. We would repeat this scenario over and over.

So, when I met up with this old colleague and discussed life and philosophy like the good old days, I had a lot of fun. When I realized that this is what I needed in my life, I felt like I had regained my old self. I was simply happy that I could talk like this again. I'm sure the alcohol helped, too, but I was the one who asked him up to my place when he took me home. He seemed a bit surprised, but as we shared a glass of wine and fooled around a little, I felt a peculiar resurgence of animalistic feelings. "I am indeed a woman," I thought.

The next morning, we shook hands by the door and said our good-byes. We decided not to see each other again as long as we were married. There was a scent of danger … it was getting too hot. But I almost cried as I watched him walk away from me.

For a while afterwards, we exchanged emails. But he started seeing another married woman, and so the two of us never met again. Also, back then, I still loved my husband a lot. I was wracked with guilt. To make matters worse, it was through this guilt that I had discovered the depth of my love toward my husband, and that left a bitter aftertaste. I finally couldn't take it anymore and confessed to my husband. "I'm sorry. I cannot lie to you," I said.

My husband said, "I am shocked. I don't know if I can forgive you, but thank you for telling me. It would've hurt me even more if you had kept the truth from me."

I even thought to myself, "Maybe he does love me after all."

After some time, my husband switched jobs and went into TV production, just as I had asked. For a while, he seemed happy; his income rose and he regained confidence in himself. On the other hand, his attitude toward me changed. He was becoming arrogant.

I was a homemaker at the time, so I made him lunches to take to work, and naturally, I took care of our home. But one morning, when I asked him to take the garbage on his way out, he responded angrily: "You're asking a person who's going to work to take out the garbage?"

I could not live this kind of life anymore, so I decided to find work myself. Our income stabilized, but the chasm between us grew wider.

There were things I wanted to do. Whether it was theater work or going to graduate school, there were challenges I could have undertaken on my own after I graduated from college. But I was scared of taking that first step toward realizing a dream. I was scared of failure. I'm beginning to think that's why I got married: it was the path right in front me.

At the same time, I started to feel the itch. I wanted to test the waters again, explore the go-getter part of me, the active and free part of me. I'd had a late start, but I'll try once again, just for myself, I thought.

I was on a mission. I contacted all my old acquaintances, inquiring about theater work. There was no shame or pride there, just a pure desire to get back into theater.

Around that time, I was asked if I would be interested in being in a play. It was not exactly the kind of production I aspired to be in, and my part was very small. But at this point, those things didn't matter as long as I could get my foot in the door. Being a small theater company, it paid virtually nothing. Four, five months thereafter, I practically lived there. I just worked hard everyday.

It was around this time that I met my next lover. Having the stage as a workplace is truly unusual. When you spend a lot of time working at a place like that, you share tremendous experiences. Our shared love of the theater brought us together in the first place, and within this natural setting we bonded as male and female. I felt very fulfilled those several months we spent together.

I started entertaining the vague notion of divorce around this time, so I felt no guilt. After the play, I said to him, "I think I'm going to get a divorce. I want to continue seeing you."

But he wouldn't listen. He was single, and said that he "could not stay in a relationship with a married woman." That made sense. I decided not to pursue it any further.

Coming home was like descending from a world of the extraordinary to the mundane. A contaminated marriage and an encingly complicitous relationship with my husband quietly awaited me. When you go this far, the more troubled the relationship, the stronger the bond. It is a chain reaction of defeat.

The second winter of our marriage, I was practically deranged. I was constantly exploding at the slightest provocation from my husband, ripping the bedding into shreds, throwing dishes. I was hysterical all the time. But, as soon as I calmed down a little, my husband would be snoring away. Of course, I couldn't get to sleep, so I felt the anger bubbling up inside of me as I watched the peaceful look on my husband's face. There were a few times when I was struck by an urge to strangle him.

More than a year had passed since we had stopped having sex. "Maybe that's because I am not clean." Thoughts like this made me feel as if all the problems that lay between us were my fault. And then I would see visions of myself hanging from a rope around my neck or saying "amen" and begging to God on my knees. It was completely neurotic.

Neurotics often get comments like, "You're overanalyzing" or "Stop whining." This is very cruel. Neurotics cannot help themselves from over-analyzing. Otherwise, it feels like escapism. "Nothing changes because I keep running away from it" or "All this is my fault." These undefinable, guilt-ridden thoughts had a stranglehold on me. It was a nightmare. I just wanted to be liberated from them.

It was especially difficult on nights when I was alone. I had already broken up with the man from the theater, but at night, I would go right up to his house on my bicycle. I didn't knock. I stood there in a daze, watching the lights from his house, and then I would go home. On cold evenings, when the winter sky looked especially beautiful, I felt deep sorrow. But if you ask me if I had loved this man that much, I would have to say that I am not so sure. In fact, when I met him again long after we broke up, I laughed to myself. Why did I fall for him? I wonder if I was just trying to run away.

My marriage at this point was beyond repair; my husband was insisting on not staying together. Still, I began to think that our love for each other would help us overcome anything. But I guess I was tired. Tired to the bones like an invalid. All I wanted to do was rest and sleep a lot. That's how I ended up at my parents' place. My parents were surprised at the sight of their emaciated daughter.

At first, all I thought about was how to start over with my husband. But as time wore on, and I gained composure, I knew for sure that I could no longer be with him.

I think I overestimated my inner strength. When I went to my parents' house, I was drained – just a shell of the person

I used to be. The sacrifices I had made in this marriage were too huge to quantify … My husband, on the other hand, didn't change one bit. He is selfish and guarded, and yet he does not fight when he has to. When he sees problems, he pretends not to see them. My feelings toward him were two-pronged: love and despair. In the end, I chose to extinguish whatever love I had for him once and for all.

Several months after I left home, I began doing some administrative work. Our divorce hadn't gone through yet, but I was eager to start anew. It was there, too, that I found a new love.

He seemed to show an interest in me right from the start, and I wasn't entirely ignoring him either. But we couldn't find the opportunity to strike up a conversation. We talked for the very first time two weeks after I joined the company. It happened at the second bar I went to with my colleagues from work.

In the taxi heading home, he slid into the same car. He was forty-three. We were years apart, but he was youthful and skilled at his job. I'm sure he had an ulterior motive. But I am always the one to make the first move. So, to be consistent, I said, "I'm getting off at your house. Stop the taxi at your place."

He hesitated as he unlocked the door. "You are married, aren't you?" He appeared a bit confused.

I said, "Yes. Obviously, this is heavy stuff, so I'm going home" and turned to go. But he stopped me and let me in. At this point, I was sure about getting a divorce, so I didn't feel like I was betraying my husband.

The divorce was official several months later. I had not seen my husband since I moved out of our house, but I met him just once to discuss our divorce. And when I met him, I realized that I still liked him. We still had feelings for each other. But there was no turning back. I knew it was all over when the words, "This is it," came out of my mouth.

I admit being in a new relationship at the time helped me

emotionally. However, the new relationship had nothing to do with my decision to get a divorce. I was not even considering a future with this man, anyway.

With the divorce being final, I have started attending a theater school on the side while doing administrative work. Recently, I landed a role with a large theater company. I feel like I am finally moving forward, albeit in baby steps. I am still dating the man I was seeing over a year ago while I was going through the divorce. All I wanted back then was somebody to lean on, so I'm surprised at this happy ending. The truth is, I began to see who he really was as we continued dating.

He has everything my husband couldn't give me: financial support, tolerance, stability and good conversation. I truly have a good time with him. That is very important, isn't it?

As for sex, the man I am seeing now says, "Everybody is a little embarrassed about it; you can do as you please. You've got to tell me what you want me to do." I feel so much more liberated in that respect. While I was married, my husband's attitude toward sex had a negative effect on me; I saw it as something disdainful. But sex is really a form of communication, the moment you know, plain and simple, that you are being loved. Sex shouldn't be quantified in terms of how many times per week for married couples, but when it disappears completely, you start suspecting your husband's feelings for you. I am a woman, and I want to be loved. My ex-husband did not give me that sense of security.

I recently quit my administrative work, moved and have decided to gamble on full-time theater work. I am a little nervous, but very fulfilled.

My boyfriend, however, appears to be in the marrying mode. He has prepared a room for me in his recently purchased condo so that I can move in anytime. But marriage is still too burdensome for me.

One thing I learned from the divorce is, never lie to yourself. If there is something you want to do, you have to fight for it. You can't just put a lid on your feelings.

I am not completely satisfied with myself. But I want to take risks and responsibilities. He is financially comfortable and supporting me would be an easy thing for him to do. And if I took refuge in that now, it would be like being under the protection of my parents; it's defeatist.

Because of my age, I may appear anxious about marriage, but in marriage, you can't be selfish. I want to be able to take his happiness into consideration. For now, I want to test my own strength.

I have strayed a number of times, I admit, but my husband was my one true love. In retrospect, those sorts of relationships wouldn't have happened under normal circumstances. I was starved for a relationship, and I sought one without a quotidian smell, a way out of this loneliness. The affairs gave me that, in a way, but they also served to remind me of my husband's existence.

In my case, I also felt strong emotions bordering on vengeance: hatred for his refusal to touch me, to communicate with me, and despair for not being loved. I think all these negative feelings took form as revenge, not necessarily against my husband, but against myself.

When we divorced, my husband said, "That was difficult for me to forgive. But I accepted it." Having an extramarital affair is out of bounds for him – something he probably could never understand.

We did have a very deep bond. Sometimes I wonder if I will ever find a greater love. I know that sounds strange, considering how painful it was. After all, we were partners in crime. No matter how tough our married life was, I still loved my husband. I cannot justify what I did. It was betrayal. I was too young, too self-absorbed to be able to let our love grow after we got married.

BLIND ALLEYS
akuma sho

ONE RIPE AVOCADO, two slabs of fresh *toro* tuna belly from the fishmonger, four expensive but tasty beef tomatoes, a bunch each of basil, *shiso* and rocket and five-hundred grams of quality Sasanishiki white rice populate my shopping list. I already have a refrigerator crammed with exotic green leaves no one had even heard of until five years ago.

Most Japanese wouldn't dare mix rice with salad, but I was no longer playing by the rules. I quit my job nine months ago at the height of summer, and I've been readjusting ever since. Ostensibly, I'm a writer "pursuing my own interests," which means I'm supposed to be working on becoming the next Haruki Murakami or Kenzaburo Oe.

Scratch that – I'm not really too fond of Oe. He strikes me as being wonderfully talented in the way, say, a prima ballerina is, but – just as most ignorami like me would rather puke their guts up than spend four hours with all those stuffed shirts at a ballet – I tend to read Oe with an ugly "so what" lurking at the back of my mind. I'll settle for Murakami and his wind-up birds for now.

Maybe, I'm fooling myself, but at least I no longer have to suffer that irresistible downward suction that I felt more keenly with each day at the office. It had grown more insistent with each passing month, tugging at my sleeves and trouser hems like some life-destroying Coriolis effect, sucking me inexorably towards the plughole of becoming a company man forever.

Vague aspirations aside, the new arrangement suits our thirty-something, no-children-likely domesticity. My wife goes out to work at eight; I start at noon. I say "start," but really, I merely commence thinking about what to feed myself in front of the television and what to put on the evening's dinner table. I tend not to put too much into lunch when it's just for me, often preferring a local eatery or coffee and half a pack of cigarettes at worst. Evening's always important, though, hence the special effort with the salad.

In the last year, I've sold just two sizeable articles: a short story for a literary venture my friend was starting (the pay was "deferred," as they say in the business) and a piece for a weekly magazine on Tokyo's sex shops. The magazine piece was due to bring home a chunk of bacon sufficient to justify my master plan of earning a crust from magazine work while writing my way to the Nobel Prize. It had been chastening work, but at least it was *my* work.

The magazine gig was yet another in a long line of reasons to be grateful to my wife – she'd put me in touch with an Obuchi-san, one of the editors at a new magazine from the publisher she did design work for. She didn't know much about the new title, but reckoned the editor would be happy not to have to deal with some flaky unknown. She was right – It had been an easy sell. I joined Obuchi for dinner one night, and he commissioned me for a chunky six-thousand worder. The sensitivity of the subject led me to ask him not to go into too much detail should he bump into my wife anytime soon.

I don't actually know why people lap up those kiss-and-tell tales of the modern city dweller's addiction to paid-for sex, but even the less-well-researched pieces can be sold with little effort to an editor somewhere. I even know journalists who write about nothing else.

For my piece, I'd not really had a great deal of research to do, having access to a wealth of friends and associates who are living encyclopedias of all things perverse. I also have a degree of personal experience to draw on. It's more or less impossible to grow up in Tokyo and go through the entire education system to age twenty-one without learning about these things firsthand. Nonetheless, I still put myself through the trouble of interviewing guys as they went about their business and visiting a dozen or so shops in Shinjuku, Shibuya and Shin-Okubo to get up to speed. A reporter frequenting prostitutes in the name of a story might seem excessive, but the weeklies like to claim the inside line and have us actually road-test the girls.

Sitting there naked from the waist down was making me nervous. I'd been hitting street touts for the lowdown on their joints and plumped for Zeminaru, Shinjuku's foremost academy of sin. Now, squeezed into a sweltering cubicle awaiting the, ahem, head girl's entrance, I'd started to get cold feet. ◆ It's not like I was some kind of newcomer to "the hobby," but my first trip in ten years to a pink salon was freaking me out. They run the damn things like they're selling donuts and coffee, not bareback blowjobs and mutual rimming. I'd chosen my slightly chubby-looking girl upfront from a photo menu, sat in a corridor with three other guys and now found myself on a white plastic wicker-like chair waiting my turn. ◆ I could hear assorted slurps and murmurs as the other punters received the pleasure they'd paid for in adjacent boltholes and – had I really wanted to – could have peered over the chest-high partition to watch the fun. Instead, feeling a stranger in a very strange land, I'd focused on getting my engine warmed up. ◆ Sex shop time isn't like regular time. It's probably similar to time spent in a dentist's office – another place that specializes in filling cavities – the way it stretches into infinity when you're waiting. After either five minutes or five hours, my prepaid pro put her head round the door and laughed gently. She probably hadn't expected my boy-scout-like preparedness, but, still, it broke the ice nicely. ◆ She was as professional in her work as just about every other Japanese is in theirs, and thirty minutes later I was back on the street, a few thousand yen and a squirt of DNA poorer, a chunk of story and a delightful lattice print on my ass richer.

Just after three and I'm still rooted to the sofa, still smoking cheap Seven Stars cigarettes, still watching a man in a yellow lion outfit roll a pair of giant dice on television. I assume it's a man in there, but it could easily be a woman or perhaps a real lion kitted out in an undignified yellow costume. To be

honest, though, I'm not that into the lion. Although giving
the illusion of watching, I'm really pondering the semiotics of
today's other main time-waster – a show featuring a panel of
housewives commenting on the season's vogue for bright print
on summer dresses.

The telephone bell shakes me from my CRT reveries, and
the hour tells me it's certain to be my wife calling for a few
pleasantries before she gets back to work. I'm not in the mood
for some reason – perhaps the unusually early heat is to blame
– and let it ring itself into exhaustion.

Realistically, it's a little too late to make myself anything
if I'm to get some work done and avoid pissing away the entire
day, so I opt to combine a shopping trip with a quick bite at my
favorite curry restaurant. Indian is a relative newcomer to the
Kunitachi restaurant scene, but aren't almost all restaurants in
almost every town? Given the baffling Mobius strip of refur-
bish, restructure and reinvent, it's getting to be a full-time job
just establishing a favorite in the first place.

Indian's resident owner/chef is an odd character. Oyama-
san rarely says a word to anyone beyond the regulation "welcome" and "thank you for coming." At school, the soberest
guys were always called Oyama; you know, the sort that goes
on to manage a prize-winningly efficient convenience store
or a country branch of a life-insurance agency. Consequently,
I'd learned to take an instant dislike to that kind of drone, but
this guy is something else. He's just so … well I know it sounds
trite, but he's so very serious about his curry.

The menu runs to only about half a dozen varieties with
large helpings, boiled or raw eggs the only variations permis-
sible, but he puts his everything into each dish, stirring the two
huge pans with his curry oar, working his material stoically
like Big Chief No Bull Here. His long black ponytail somehow
lends gravitas to his earnestness. He even uses the back of the
menu to explain his philosophy:

"This is just a small shop with two gas rings, so we can't

produce large quantities of curry. Since each batch takes three days to prepare, we sometimes run out and have to close early. Please understand."

I go through my usual charade of politely considering all the options before ordering my usual mushroom curry with a boiled egg split neatly in two.

In some ways, I envy his dedication to the cause. It seems like little else matters to him beyond his house of curry, but of course no one's that simple. The distance between strangers adds a grass-is-always-greener filter, even to the curry man.

At the old-fashioned shopping arcade, I breeze efficiently from store to store picking up the ingredients for my salad. The only thing I can't get is rocket, but I'm well covered in the greens department anyway. I could go to the huge new Seiyu supermarket, but it's pretty expensive and, given a choice, I don't see why anyone should fail to support his local traders.

Shopping is the one vital aspect of everyday life that I still plan reasonably coherently. But today I skip the only grocer in town who keeps rocket when I catch a glimpse in there of a woman I had an affair of sorts with.

It happened three years ago, when I'd been married for less than a year, and spanned no more than half a dozen muggy afternoons at the peak of the rainy season. I'd been spending my days at home then too, recovering from pretty serious pneumonia rather than giving in to terminal sloth as now.

She was quite a bit older than me, but Mrs. Robinson she wasn't. Nothing beyond the usual deceit and regret went on – we met (while shopping of course), fumbled guiltily with each other a few times and parted company feeling considerably worse for the experience. Between beginning and end, I'd shared little of myself and such a short time later retain few memories of events beyond endless hours listening to her self-recrimination mixed with interminable sobbing as she clung to me and poured out years of loneliness.

Late morning Kabukicho may be a touch on the quiet side, but it's great for seekers of discount action, my next doctoral field. ◆ The desk staff at Hinomaru were more like hall monitors than pimps. I half expected to be forced to carry a wooden pass if I needed a leak. Given their fixed smiles, maybe they'd work out well at some airline. ◆ "Sir, will that be screwing or non-screwing? With or without anal?" ◆ "Thankyouverymuch, pleasetakeyourseatandenjoythetrip." ◆ Fat chance. Fat girls too, but I'd managed to wring a few pearls from one of the legit customers – something about the state of the economy being a blessing for sex shoppers like him, as it drove prices down and forced the women in the business to try that much harder. ◆ "Customer loyalty is back with a bang," he told me.

I always derive an enormous sense of well-being from the walk between the east side of town, where the old shopping street is, and our place near Yaho station at the northern edge of town. It takes in the entire length of Daigaku Dori, which is, in my opinion, by far the most attractive avenue in Tokyo.

Because of the warm weather – it's only mid-April, yet the thermometer has already risen to twenty-seven degrees – the blossoms on the cherry trees have given up the ghost and are committing suicide en masse. It's an odd way to think of *sakura*, but it's an image that's been taking up valuable brain time since the real suicides started six weeks ago.

This is Tokyo, so people doing themselves in isn't even news usually, but the papers have been filled since late winter with stories of folk getting together in cozy little suicide pacts. Groups of three or four complete strangers have been hooking up online, buying charcoal stoves as per the guidelines on the same site and driving off to someplace quiet to gas themselves. Most of them couldn't even be bothered to leave notes behind.

I'm sitting on one of the municipal benches that dot the avenue, thinking how those morons – they'd have to be morons, wouldn't they? – were missing out on one of the best, albeit shortest, *sakura* seasons in years and wondering why I'm so damn happy. A light breeze rustles the trees, and the petals snow down in a pink and white blizzard. One of them lands plum on the tip of my cigarette, evaporating in an instant.

Even with the presence of the yammering local-election candidates atop their sound trucks, this is far too pleasant for someone who's supposed to be a starving artist in his garret banging out classics.

Perhaps the ingrate's equation my life has become reads something like:

$$(Complacency \times Inertia) \ \frac{Creative\ Drive + Career\ Risk}{Supportive\ Wife} = \begin{matrix} Going \\ Nowhere \\ Fast \end{matrix}$$

Even so, I don't struggle trying to understand such dark matter; I just accept it and relax a little more.

"Sixty nine, please wait in line," should've been the motto of the place near the 109 department store on Dogenzaka. Instead, they just put up a sign with a stupid name: Loose Socks. It's a reference to the baggy white socks worn by schoolgirls – the Holy Grail of gropers. The crew taking the dough front of house were as efficient as the previous bunch, but my unease at the seediness of the place convinced me I could feel their beady eyes drilling through the back of my head. The schoolgirl rape-fetish porno on the dust-encrusted reception-hall television ratcheted the tension a notch closer to embolic, and I half expected an Invasion of the Body Snatchers *point-and-shriek moment when they discovered I was a real human being. Dedicated journo that I am, I managed to stick it out. ◆ In spite of the sick videos and the less-than-wholesome specialty, the women on call were generally friendly and mostly human, but since I didn't feel up to much with either of the two girls sent into the stinking hot room,*

and the school gear made me feel like the very embodiment
of evil, we just chatted a little about their simmering resent-
ment of the recent influx of South American whores and how
all the world was against them anyway.

As usual, a rogue's gallery of leaflets has found its way
into my mailbox in the two hours I've been away. Turn your
back and you're likely to be lost under a tsunami of fliers for
pizza delivery and massage parlors. The brochures declaring
the benefits of some new apartment block round the corner always tickle me. "Your place sucks – why not move here?"

The lock gives an arthritic squeak as I force the key upon
it. It's a good sign that the dryness of winter is on the back foot;
even mechanical things need to get used to the change in the
weather.

I need to make a few seasonal adjustments, too – cutting
back on smoking would be a start. I actually just took it up to
give me something to do and to add to the bohemian image,
but I think I prefer drinking excessively to giving myself can-
cer. No matter – now I'm home, food's on my mind.

In most movies that feature a cooking scene, the cook
conducts his or her culinary symphony holding a glass of red
wine in one of those ridiculously long-stemmed glasses. We all
know no one has that kind of glassware at home, probably not
even the fabulous Oe-san. I, on the other hand, am disciplined
and don't need alcohol to cook to.

I start with the greens – the leaves are certainly better
than any others on the tables of western Tokyo, but rocket's bitterness would have helped. I'm not one of these pretentious
types who buys food for its novelty value – I genuinely can't get
enough of Belgian endive, escarole, spinach, watercress and the
like. I count them off, rinsing carefully as I check for any that
have rebelled against captivity and reverted to that almost-liq-
uid state some salad vegetables tend toward.

Basil, *shiso* and assorted dried herbs consume about

ten seconds as I shred and shake them into the leaf mix. The chunky beef tomatoes smell so sweet when I have their guts exposed, I have to dice and add half a red onion to offset the overpowering sensation they'll bring to the salad.

Next comes the *toro*. It's the kind of ingredient that looks impressive, especially when it's a slob like me doing the cooking, but it's really a no-brainer. Its succulent fleshiness lends a touch of glamour to the finished dish, so I throw it in everything. My wife likes to joke that it'll be on my cornflakes next.

Out with the best knife and slice the *toro* into quarter-inch cubes, then set those aside to dump on top later. Here's a secret – if you want to keep your *toro* looking juicy, you can cheat and stick it in the icebox for ten minutes. When the ice crystals burst after a minute or so at room temperature, they make the fish look like it jumped straight out of the sea and onto the plate.

Finally, the best part of any salad – the avocado. I'm frequently told I'm so European for daring to have learned other languages and liking avocado, but what's not to like? It looks like a hand grenade and feels like leather on the outside, but, when ripe, its meat is as soft as melting chocolate, the whole delicious package orbiting that beautiful brown pit at its core.

This one looks promising, but I'm fully aware how deceptive avocados can be. I slip its skin off and snick away a dark spot right where the stalk once joined the fruit to the tree. As I pare off the meat, I begin to get a bad feeling. Sure enough, a black seam pollutes the flesh the entire length of the stone. What's left when I'm finished will taste good enough, and I'll get over the loss of the dark parts – no really, I will – but it always seems such a waste when that happens.

Like most of the other dumps I visited, I'd found Shibuya's Seiki 21 on one of those review websites run by nerds with too much time on their hands and too little personality to find a not-for-profit life partner. They were pretty thorough, though, and saved me a deal of shoe leather. Good reports about the friendliness of the girls at Seiki 21 suggested it might provide some solid material. ♦ Mika came as a recommendation from one of the otaku *geeks as a hooker who gave a "great GFE." That's aficionado talk for "girlfriend experience," an English phrase they use, meaning she has a reputation for treating her Johns slightly better than dirt. Just as well, since I intended to give her a good talking to. ♦ Before I had a chance to, she got straight to it, stripping off immediately and getting right back to basics. Do not pass go. Do not collect two-hundred dollars. Go straight to jail. It would have been rude to refuse. ♦ Afterwards, she said I had fifteen minutes left and sauntered off to fetch me a cold beer from somewhere in the dark corridor. She was clearly under twenty – not yet old enough to drink the beer, but wise enough to realize the control she had. ♦ "How come you do this kind of work?" I asked when she came back, still completely nude. I wanted to get her on my side, but wasn't sure where to start. "You're great at this, but you must know, you could get a normal job, like in a shop or something." ♦ "I enjoy it," was her response, strangely expected. ♦ "And it is a normal job – my parents aren't stupid, they know I work here. If they're not bothered, why should I be? Besides, where else can I get paid extra just because some* shimei *asks for me by name?" ♦ Not that I wanted it any other way, but that's all I was to her – a guy who had a* shimei, *a request. Giggling behind her hand, she explained that it netted her an extra two-thousand yen on top of her basic fee. ♦ "I get even more when I take the boss used tissues and prove I satisfied old Mr. Shimei." ♦ I shifted uncomfortably, feeling both guilty and dirty in the company of this skinny little girl. ♦ "It's hardly difficult work, is it?" she added with the air of one who knows she's won the debate.*

At six, I switch on the NHK radio news to catch the headlines. Business BS isn't news, as far as I'm concerned, so I turn to the rice. The Sasanishiki strain requires five rinses – that's at least two more than regular white rice – which it gets in surprisingly cold water that numbs my hand after the fourth cycle. The year's new heat has yet to penetrate the ground to where the pipes lie. After, I dump the pristine grains in our Zojirushi-brand rice cooker – one modern gadget I could never do without.

On the table, I set out two pairs of good chopsticks on matching ceramic rests we bought on an *onsen* vacation in Kyushu and a placemat for the salad bowl. I'll bring the salad out of the fridge twenty minutes before we eat to add oil, vinegar and a sprinkling of dried seaweed to give it bite. A pair of non-movie wine glasses and two white plates complete the setting.

The phone rings again, and I motivate myself sufficiently to lift the receiver this time. My wife asks if she can bring anything, but warns that she could be twenty minutes late. I tell her everything's fine and I'm behaving myself.

Resuming my position on the sofa, my good fortune to have her even bother to ask comes to mind for the umpteenth time this week. I constantly think how lucky I am after my indiscretions. Sure, I'd owned up to that store-struck affair as a specimen charge (the professional transgressions don't count, do they?) and plea-bargained my way to where we are now, but I can't help picturing myself as the black muck in her otherwise perfect avocado.

Of all the interviews I did for that feature article, Mika had been the most difficult, not because she was aggressive or spaced out, but because she'd been so resigned to her lot. ◆ Most of the guys I'd spoken to were just out for some throwaway fun – they genuinely didn't give it any more thought beyond simply getting laid. In fact, half of them ended up in knocking shops because their boss was "treating" them. The other half needed to be seen as being as misogynistic as their peers. Undercover journalism is an extreme example, but it's pretty typical among Japanese my age to be so matter-of-fact about sexual transactions, and I've even had more than one overseas friend tell me it's top of their list of reasons why Japanese women deserve well-hung, big-nosed white guys. ◆ *Mika's story wasn't the typical roll call of abuse and familial estrangement. Rather, it was all about a total lack of ambition. She'd never tried in school, couldn't be bothered with all the polite bowing and scraping required to work in even the lowest convenience store and had fallen into the sex trade simply by virtue of some of the similarly lazy people she hung out with.* ◆ *I know ninety-nine percent of girls these days might look like hookers, but they're mostly harmless – typically, they're content with a "proper job" somewhere or other, drinking too much on weekends while dating a succession of similar-looking guys in suits until a bell goes off in their heads and they marry one of them. Then, it's time to pack it all in for a life of sitting at home, shopping and making dinner.* ◆ *Not Mika. She chose to spend her days sucking cock by the yard for six-thousand yen a pop in a booth at the back of a strip joint.* ◆ *After Seiki 21, a depression had come over me, leaving* me *feeling like the prostitute, completing my research scurrying around from pink salon to fashion health and image club to bikini studio, rounding up the latest in disposable flesh fads. A sort of soiled Kobo Daishi performing my own take on the Shikoku pilgrimage.* ◆ *Aside from the traditional sex shops, the final draft of my feature took in streetwalkers, their pimps and the Chinese mafia's gang wars with the local* yakuza. *Feeling pretty uncharitable toward muckraking journalism in general, I also devoted space to debunking the* puchi-iede *"phenomenon" some of the press had conjured up about junior-high schoolers skipping classes to sell themselves for next to nothing and a few Louis Vuitton accessories.* ◆ *I topped it off with a detailed chart of the going rates for* honban, *or full sex, and* nama fera, *the oral option most establishments favor, throughout each of Tokyo's so-called red-light districts. I hit the send button with a rare distaste for a writer with a hefty check coming his way.*

"One last cigarette," I tell myself, then I'll open the windows to clear the cancerous fog away. My wife doesn't like smoking, and I basically agree with her. It's been a full day, so I treat myself to an Ebisu beer and a few minutes with *number9dream*, the novel I'm halfway through, to go with the smokes. A winning combination for sure.

First I check the clock. It's after seven already, so I try her mobile for reassurance that I haven't already been abandoned, but it just rings through to the answering machine. I mumble a message about dinner and return to my book. Although he knows us well for a foreigner, I can't concentrate on Mitchell's demanding style, and the gloom invading from outside is making reading a strain anyway. The Ebisu goes down a lot easier.

Flicking on the TV is less demanding than getting up to hit the lights, so I pick up the remote almost automatically. From the seven channels of carefully targeted garbage, I settle on something vacuous about European lifestyles and let images of rolling fields and big, happy families wash over me. Within a few minutes I hit the mute button to silence the moronic female *tarento* showing us round Switzerland. Unsurprisingly, it has a soporific effect, and I start to nod off.

When I awake, the TV screen is blank, and I initially think I must have slept right through to closedown. It's a pleasant, fuzzy feeling for a second or two until I notice it's actually been turned off and then glance around the room to see my wife in her usual place at the table.

She's already dressed for bed with a robe on and has done that towel turban thing with her hair. I sit up, rubbing my eyes and noticing that the apartment smells of *yuzu* lemons – like a bath has been run.

"I didn't want to wake you," she says. "You were sleeping

so soundly, I figured it'd been a tough day, so I let you sleep on."

"Mm, yeah," I reply.

She moves over to the sofa and nudges me so she can sit. She leans in and plants a soft kiss on my sleep-lined cheek, then hands me two freezing cold beers. I open one, hand it to her and repeat the motion on the second can for myself.

"Sorry I'm so late, but I had a pretty heated meeting with Obuchi-san over at the magazine."

"And? My name didn't come up, did it?"

"In a way. It's not looking so good down there for him. Seems the magazine isn't going to publish even one more issue. Something to do with a threat of libel action hanging over one of their first big stories."

The implications are obvious, even to me.

"You know, this probably means you won't get paid," she adds, unnecessarily.

"At least the other divisions are unaffected and we've got my salary, so you've still got time to … "

It's not the best time to be planning our future, and she knows it. I feel a chill setting in.

"I'll use that bathwater while it's still hot," I tell her after a couple of motionless minutes, more as an excuse to stop what I'm hearing than anything else.

Looking at the *yuzu* bobbing in the green bathwater, millimeters from my nose, I wonder how many more dead ends I'm going to charge down, how many more days I'm going to waste in pursuit of something I can barely identify.

My wife slides the shutter door open and looks in on me, probably to check that I haven't opened a vein.

"Are you okay? I'm going to turn myself in now," she says, quoting one of my favorite dumb English gags. I nod and force a weak half smile.

"Thanks," she adds, withdrawing to leave me with my citric mood.

"The salad was perfect, by the way."

SAN MAN DOWN
cal ranson

S HE HAD PLANNED IT JUST SO. They would find the car at just the right time – not too late, not, heaven forbid, too early. They – it didn't matter who – would convey the news to the ones who wouldn't listen.

She rolled the window to the top as he put a flame to the charcoal. He, tall and thin, with a face even a mother would turn from, swallowed his handful of sleeping pills greedily. She considered, then dismissed, the idea of slipping hers in a pocket. It had to look like a genuine attempt, after all, if she were to make her point. Down in one with a gulp of *ocha*.

"Are you sure that window's tight?" he asked her.

"As a drum," she replied, failing to fake a match for his enthusiasm.

She hesitated, wondering what was appropriate conversation for two people in a car parked on a lonely track with the seats reclined all the way.

"Um, do you want to hold hands?" she asked him in an odd cross of pity and uncertainty.

"I'd rather not, if you don't mind. We barely know each other, right?"

"I'm fine either way," she lied, her voice betraying her.

Fair enough – they were courting death, not one another.

Truth be told, she was terrified something would go wrong and she'd die too quickly. He only feared something would go wrong and he'd end up with a pumped stomach, a splitting headache and yet another failure to add to the list. At least, that's what she'd drawn from the handful of short emails they'd exchanged in the previous two weeks.

One of those "so what?" statistics kept coming back to her: *san man nin*, thirty-thousand people. That's how many dumbasses did themselves in every year in Japan, most of them hanged by the neck or minced under trains. Thirty-thousand scared, selfish fools. She lay back, turning the numbers and methods over in her mind, meditating upon what drove that mad rush into nothingness. Not that it wasn't obvious to her or any other nineteen-year-old.

Carbon monoxide added to sleeping pills made it as easy as dozing off and removed the risk of puking the drugs up. It was even becoming quite a popular method, thanks to the *jisatsu keijiban* Internet bulletin boards sprouting over cyberspace like *shiitake* on a cowpat.

The papers were full of it – so far this year, more than two dozen people under twenty-five had hooked up with strangers online and headed off somewhere quiet to lie down and die in a car with a charcoal brazier on the back seat. A life of loneliness, somehow redeemed by ending it in company.

Anyway, what was her excuse? She was just making a point – that was why she'd suggested Kamikuishiki village in Yamanashi Prefecture, where the only poor-sap losers of the season had been found and dragged from their rented car into a life of shame and recrimination, and the locals were on a town-hall mandated suicide lookout. She didn't tell him that, but he hardly spoke anyway, apparently just grateful for her answering his electronic solicitation for a quiet, serious partner in death.

Road trip to nowhere – I'm male, in my twenties and have had enough. I'm looking for a driving companion with own vehicle.

Earnest only, please. Gender irrelevant. Tokyo area. Email: chocobunnychan@docomo.ne.jp

One thing he did let slip was that he liked the village's proximity to Mount Fuji's notorious Aokigahara suicide forest and the fact that the Aum Shinrikyo cult had brewed their sarin there in preparation for gassing half of Tokyo.

"Those woods are just so passé anyway – we're too young to do it in there," he'd said, almost as if he was thumbing his nose at the nation's second-best-loved end-it-yourself hangout just around the corner.

She closed her eyes when the CO started to build up, thinking about the only better-known site – Nikko's Kegon Falls, and the teenaged Misao Fujimura, who'd started it all a hundred years ago. A student of Soseki Natsume, he couldn't accept the ineluctable futility of being and carved a precocious *tetsugakuteki jisatsu*, or philosophical suicide, note on a tree before dashing himself on the rocks one sunny May early last century. Fujiwara's elegant prose read, "Ultimate despair and ultimate hope are one and the same."

"Pretty deep for a kid, eh?" she absent-mindedly mumbled.

He started to reply, but obviously thought better of it and just grunted. She was relieved, not feeling much like broadening her thoughts to encompass him more than she had to.

She felt heavy and wondered how long it would be before someone arrived.

Her brother had screamed at her on the phone, something about being a selfish bitch, but she knew he'd call the police, who would send someone. She'd certainly dropped enough hints about how to find her. The ridiculous old suv she'd requisitioned from her mom wouldn't be hard to spot out there in the sticks either.

Just in case, she lugubriously lifted her wet sandbag of a hand to the window roll. It seemed to have become stiffer in the fifteen minutes since she'd wound it up so eagerly.

He was snoring in great watery bursts now, irritating her intensely as she struggled to raise herself for better leverage. Nothing was moving outside.

Inside, the warm leather sucked her ever downwards into the comfort of the driver's seat. Resigned, she gave up for now and slid back into its softness. Maybe a refreshing nap would bring her strength back, if only she could be sure to wake up in time.

"If only … " How many times had she heard that before?

CANNED COFFEE
david cady

Japan Tobacco

Name comes from company's goal of using technology and know-how to become the origin, or "roots," of a new type of coffee.

The "Waist Wave" can shape is a signature of the Roots series.

Company:	Japan Tobacco
Brand:	Roots "Real Blend"
Style:	high-temperature, short-time method
Motto:	depth, clean finish, aroma
Beans:	blended with Brazil Santos

Fuller-bodied and more bitter than many other blends. Kevin Costner and Brad Pitt claim to like it. For maximum satisfaction, drink this while watching music video clips on the jumbo-screen TV across the street as you wait for the light to change.

HOT POINT

MANY WESTERN MOVIE STARS AND ATHLETES HAVE HAWKED CANNED COFFEE IN JAPAN. ROOTS HAS COSTNER AND PITT ON ITS SIDE. WONDA HAS BEEN PRAISED BY TIGER WOODS. BRUCE WILLIS HAS TAKEN A STAND FOR GEORGIA BRAND COFFEES. AND MARIAH CAREY HAS STUMPED FOR NESCAFE. IN FACT, WESTERNERS GET PAID RIDICULOUS SUMS TO DO HIGH-PROFILE ADS IN JAPAN THAT ARE NEVER BROADCAST OUTSIDE THE COUNTRY. THE MOVIE *LOST IN TRANSLATION* IS ABOUT AN AGING AMERICAN MOVIE STAR DOING WHISKEY COMMERCIALS IN JAPAN. BILL MURRAY, THE STAR OF THE FILM, HAS BEEN QUOTED AS SAYING THAT HE BASED HIS PERFORMANCE ON ADVERTISING DONE IN JAPAN BY HARRISON FORD AND COSTNER. "THEY BOTH LOOKED EXACTLY THE SAME," MURRAY SAID, "AS IF THEY WERE PRAYING THAT NO ONE WOULD SEE THOSE ADS IN WISCONSIN."

named after a port in Colombia where a French trader introduced coffee seedlings

"one-hundred percent Colombian beans"

"coffee"

Company:	Nestle Japan Group
Brand:	Santa Marta X
Style:	split roast
Motto:	a traditional coffee
Beans:	mostly hand-picked in the Sierra Nevada mountains

Chemical introductory notes give way to a pleasant bitterness and lingering ashy finish. Best suited to springtime walks between Meguro and Ebisu stations while listening to the Flaming Lips on headphones and wearing orange socks with purple polka dots in an attempt to give yourself a kooky, artistic air.

HOT POINT
THE JAPANESE DRINK
ON AVERAGE 4.29
CUPS OF INSTANT
COFFEE, 3.22 CUPS OF
REGULAR COFFEE
AND 1.77 CUPS OF
CANNED COFFEE
PER WEEK.

Red was chosen because it represents delicious taste and it is a color people feel close to.

named to attract the early morning commuter

"Morning Shot: 100% freshly harvested Arabica beans make the unique flavor. Five different levels of extremely slow roasting creates the clear taste and rich bitterness."

"Wonda morning shot coffee"

Company:	Asahi Soft Drinks
Brand:	Wonda "Morning Shot"
Style:	five-stage roast
Motto:	a wake-up call in a can
Beans:	one-hundred percent Arabica

Smells like an unchanged diaper. A tasty, straightforward brew that's less sugary than the average canned coffee. Best served warm while watching a sunrise from the summit of Mt. Fuji.

HOT POINT
ASAHI SOFT DRINKS HAD BEEN FLOUNDERING FOR YEARS UNTIL IT DECIDED TO MARKET A CANNED COFFEE SPECIFICALLY AIMED AT MORNING COMMUTERS. WONDA MORNING SHOT WAS A SMASH HIT AFTER ITS RELEASE IN 2002, ESSENTIALLY REVERSING THE COMPANY'S FORTUNES.

Boss Coffee "Fine Roast" (Suntory)
Initially redolent of saccharine and hickory, this mellows into a coffee with a soft finish and high drinkability. Good for slamming down on a humid day while striding along a tree-lined avenue achirp with cicadas.

Cafe La Mode "Bin Cho Tan" (AGF)
Once you get over the initial poopy/burning rubber smell, you'll discover a brew that nearly delivers the full-bodied taste of real coffee, albeit real coffee that has about six table-spoons of sugar in it. Perfect while squatting near a train station listening to an out-of-tune busker "do" Dylan.

DyDo Blend Coffee (DyDo)
This boisterous sugar-bomb smells and tastes like a maple bar. Should be consumed surreptitiously as a quick pick-me-up on a crowded morning commuter train.

Georgia "Ice Cafe Vanilla Limited Edition" (Coca-Cola)
A disgustingly sweet offering that tastes more like vanilla ice cream liqueur than coffee. An intriguing counterpoint to a bag of dried squid purchased at 7-Eleven.

Super Fire "Stone Wash" (Kirin)
Notes of caramel and amaretto combine nicely to offer a solid little coffee with a clean finish. Goes down well while pedaling along the neighborhood shopping street at dusk before renting a video on half-price night.

Coffee "Premium Drip" (Heartflag)
A no-frills yet flavorsome offering that doesn't try to over-whelm the taste buds. Sip on late-afternoon promenades around the Imperial Palace, making sure to appreciate the dramatic stone ramparts and haughty swans in the moat. Note that swans looks less majestic when you see their

splayed feet working furiously under the water.

Fire "Classico Standard Coffee with Naked Beans" (Kirin)
Initial band-aid overtones ease into a surprisingly smooth finish with hints of charcoal. An excellent complement to late-night cab rides home on an elevated highway winding through a massive corridor of apartment buildings and neon billboards.

Georgia "Original" (Coca-Cola)
Thin and sugary, this veteran brew is redeemed only by its nostalgic appeal and extra-tall can. An ideal companion while wandering lost in the industrial wastelands of Kawasaki and stumbling upon a street teeming with prostitutes.

Pokka Coffee "Original" (Pokka)
Extremely sweet and slightly garlicky. Brewed for peak flavor during the rainy season, while yet another torrent forces you to hunker in the doorway of a curry shop. Go ahead and order a large asparagus, tomato and cheese curry. When the rain eases, pay your bill and crack open the Pokka. The lingering spices in your mouth will mingle with the sweetness of the coffee to create a complex flavor not unlike coconut.

UCC "Original Milk & Coffee" (UCC)
Tastes like creamer with sugar. Its unapologetic treacliness works best on packed train platforms, particularly while awaiting the last train of the day at Ikebukuro station and being accosted by a drunk dwarf clutching a five-hundred-milliliter can of Kirin Lager. After the encounter, be careful not to jokingly chastise your friend for speaking with a dwarf, as this act of disrespect toward a less-advantaged (and downright tanked) member of society will horrify your girlfriend and end any chances of you "getting lucky"

that evening.[1] Of further note: Never, under any circumstances, demonstrate to your girlfriend your supposed facility with sign language, complete with slurred spoken accompaniment, even if you know through your six-Guinness haze that your rendition is jaw-droppingly accurate. Your girlfriend may turn out to have a friend whose sister is deaf, and that friend may be standing right next to your girlfriend.

Georgia "Morning Coffee" (Coca-Cola)

This acidic, low-sugar concoction tastes like coffee that's been left in the pot for a day then reheated in a microwave. Clean-lined and astringent. For best results, knock back with a grimace before telling her you need your freedom, then hop on the Inokashira line to Shibuya and get shit-faced on gin and tonics.

UCC "Sumi Yaki Coffee" (UCC)

A pleasantly disorienting interplay between sweet and bitter elements that combine to produce a hearty finish. This is a perfect post-hangover beverage that is most effective after a bowl of noodles. It should remain unopened for the first ten minutes of the walk home from the ramen shop and then be consumed in the final three. During the initial ten min-

---

[1] On the tense ride back to your place, show your defiance by becoming unnaturally interested in the act of drinking your coffee. Take in the old-school artwork on the can; really study it, every detail. Don't judge it. Rather, tilt your mind's eye quizzically askew as if saying, "Curious." Close your eyes and hold the mouth of the can up to your nose and slowly breathe in the aroma. What do you smell? Toffee? Hints of No. 2 pencil eraser? Now cup the can in both hands and slowly raise it to your lips. Drink the nectar in one short, sharp intake, allowing some air in so as to create a ragged slurp. This is how the pros drink coffee. Allow the flavors to play around on your tongue. Mentally address each one. "Hello Sweet 'N Low. Ah yes, caramel, how are you? Greetings, shit." Repeat this ritual until you reach Shinjuku station. As the doors hiss open, place the can under your seat and bolt out of the train, then turn to gloat at your flummoxed girlfriend as the doors close. You've won the battle. Now go home and fall asleep in the flickering blue light of your TV, flanked by congealed convenience-store curry and a liter bottle of Calpis Water.

utes, squeeze the can firmly as the owner of the used-record shop quickly looks up from whatever he's doing to make eye contact with you through the window as you pass by, like he always does, making you wonder for the hundredth time how in the world he knows you're there. Maybe he's thinking the same thing. Him, with his goofy-ass permed mullet. On the final leg of your journey, open the can and, while absently sipping, fantasize that you earn a million dollars for every step you take. Try to guess how many steps it will take to reach your front door. If your prediction proves accurate to within five steps, the multimillion-dollar jackpot is yours. Consider what you'd do with the money and whether it would really make you happy. Decide that you'd give large sums to friends and family, but then wonder if doing so would put weird strains on your relationships, like, would they feel obliged to always keep in touch and send Christmas cards and otherwise constantly express their gratitude? If that were the case, they might actually grow resentful of you, perhaps even only subconsciously, thus messing up what were once normal relationships. Conclude that money is a complicated thing but that in the end, being rich would be awesome.

LIFE WITH A BILINGUAL DOG
robert juppe jr.

YOU OFTEN HEAR WESTERNERS in Japan complain that friendship does not come easily. This needs qualifying: it does not come easily on *Western* terms. On buses and trains, for example, strangers seldom talk. Waiting rooms are generally peaceful, tranquil places. Packed restaurants can often appear funereal. It is not that people are not friendly; rather, there is something Confucianist going on. It is viewed as rude to break up *wa*, or harmony, in Japan. In the West, people tend to try and forge relationships with others. Here, it is assumed that harmonious relationships already exist. The aim is not to break or damage them. And the easiest way to go about this is to keep quiet and avoid contact. One of the odd by-products of this logic is the assumption that everyone around you in any organized or semi-organized setting is your friend (kids in the same class at school, colleagues in an office, homeless guys sharing the same park).

After many years in Japan, I thought that I, too, had few genuine friends (though I did not realize that they were all around me, according to the principles of Confucianism). I had tried to "go native" to as great an extent as possible, but failed in most important ways. Yet as time passed, I felt that I had at least achieved a state of *wa*. And just as people here, generally speaking, seem to like having systematic lives, my life became more neatly arranged the longer I lived here. I spent a lot of time at work and felt that I had little time for friends. In this sense, I had adapted well … until I got a real best friend. And you know from the old proverb what kind of best friend I would get.

My neatly organized life was placed in jeopardy the day my Japanese wife said she wanted a dog. She had found an abandoned puppy on the Internet and suggested that we drive out to get him. I tried to warn her that there would be hardships involved and that keeping a dog in a tiny Tokyo apartment might not be all that simple. Like a child promising a wary parent, however, she insisted that she would make the pet her top priority. I felt somewhat like Molotov probably did after Ribbentrop insisted the Nazis would never violate the non-aggression pact with the Soviets.

We drove in a rented car for seven hours to a small mountain town to fetch the homeless pup. We brought him to our home in the center of Tokyo and dubbed him "Boss." The name had nothing to do with the omnipresent brand of canned coffee sold in vending machines. My wife told me that she had thought up the name decades earlier when she had dreamed of one day having a dog. The process struck me as somewhat odd, sort of like me deciding at this very moment what I will drink with lunch one arbitrary day forty years from now.

He is a cute dog; he looks like a little fox, though he also has the misfortune of looking like a jindo, the dogs that Koreans eat. When I am sharing scraps with him from my dinner plate, I frequently remind him of his noble heritage by noting that he's lucky he did not wind up on it.

My wife certainly loved having a pet, but like a kid, she began shirking the walking duties at every opportunity. I did not mind her pretending to be asleep each morning or returning home mysteriously five minutes after I had gone out with the dog, but I had no idea that walking a dog would change my life to such an extent. For one, my *wa* was upended. Once I started walking Boss, I became Mr. Popular. Every time we hit the streets together, I was besieged with questions and comments. I was so rattled by this unexpected celebrity attention that I started taking Boss out early in the morning to avoid the general harassment. I wanted my *wa* back. I had gotten used to Japanese-style friendship. It should go without saying, too, that I wanted my wife to walk the dog more often.

Through Boss, I learned much about people's thoughts and views on language, friendship and more. Quite a few people would look at him and say, "Oh, I guess I cannot speak to him because he lives with you and won't understand Japanese." When I point out that we are conversing in Japanese and that I often talk with Boss in Japanese myself, they stare back blankly as if I were delivering a short lecture on quantum physics.

One guy I see from time to time has a beefy akita that tries to tear apart any dog he encounters; while this owner is struggling to keep his menacing mutt under control, he is constantly shouting at the dog, "He is your friend! You are friends!" I do not know how long he has been trying to convince his dog of this widespread camaraderie within the canine community, but it does not seem to have sunk in during the past two years.

On occasion, I will speak to Boss in Japanese out of habit, mainly because my wife will do so at home. It is not planned; it just seems sort of natural. "Oh, it must be hard for you," some people have said to me. "You have to talk to your dog in Japanese because you are in Japan!"

Since many people long to be bilingual here, they are frequently astonished to discover that Boss is bilingual … well, if you can call understanding five commands in English and four and a half in Japanese bilingual. In fact, nobody seems to notice that when I order Boss in a firm voice in English to lie down, he usually barks or tries to shake my hand.

Boss keeps attracting people I never expected to talk to. We were sitting on a wall one hot summer day in Ueno Park (before he became bilingual, in his puppy days) when a homeless man approached. He asked me what my dog's name was, then stared hard at Boss and said, "Boss … *Ote*!" Boss stared back at him blankly, so I said, "He can shake hands, but you have to ask him in English." The homeless guy then looked at me and asked, "How do you say '*ote*' in English?" I told him: "Shake." He looked at Boss and said, "Shok!" I repeated "shake" for him, and he said, "Shuk." This time, the little dog raised his paw very slowly and shook hands with the homeless man.

The man cracked up. He repeatedly shook hands with Boss, then scurried off into the underbrush, probably to share his cultural experience with some fellow hobos.

There were further changes in my life thanks to this little hound. One of the biggest adjustments took place during our vacations. Before Boss came along, my wife and I could be on our own during the holidays. We could stay at a Japanese inn, for example, and rarely talk to anybody except the staff. Even in the dining rooms, where sometimes as many as twenty couples gathered, never did I talk to anyone there, even though we were all ostensibly friends. It becomes very natural. You become used to filtering them out. In fact, when I travel with some of my Western friends and they decide "to get friendly" with the people around them, I feel extremely uncomfortable because they are intruding on these strangers' *wa*.

But once we had Boss, my wife began booking us at "pet pensions," inns that cater to guests with pets (they should actually be called "dog pensions." I have yet to see someone bring a raccoon or an arachnid.) At these inns, your pet can go everywhere you go, including the dining room. At the first pet pension we went to, there were small anchors in the dining room to which you could hook your dog's lead. Everybody eats a French dinner and their dogs lie at their feet. The dogs are not allowed to eat in the dining room; they are merely permitted to help reproduce a Norman Rockwell-like setting. Well, Norman Rockwell in kaleidoscope, because there are fifteen couples and fifteen dogs.

The presence of the dogs in the dining room has another big effect: people talk to one another. The dogs help break the silence barrier, but the conversations are almost exclusively focused on the dogs. This would be a typical one:

Table One:	Excuse me, so sorry to ask you a question, but what is your dog's name?
Me:	Boss. And may I have your dog's name?
Table One:	John. (*Many dogs in Japan have typical Western names that were suspiciously common in the 1950s like Bruce, Rick or Mary.*) What

	kind of dog is Boss?
Me:	He is mixed. We don't know because he was abandoned.
Table One:	Hello, Boss. *(Person from table one pets Boss.)* You were lucky, weren't you? You got picked up! *(Most of the people who frequent pet pensions are well-to-do and have expensive purebreds. Boss is kind of like the orphan among dogs at the pet pensions, just as his owner is inevitably the sole* gaijin.*)* How old is he?
Me:	Two and a half. How old is Jack?
Table One:	John!
Me:	Uh, sorry, John.
Table One:	He is three. *(To John, suddenly, in English.)* John! Stand up! *(Japanese people like to give dog commands, for some weird reason, in English. In fact, some people look uncomfortable when I speak to Boss in Japanese. Someone must have decided that dogs belong to the world of English. My wife suggests that maybe they talk to dogs in English because they feel that dogs and Americans are pretty much on the same level.)*

Wager: Pick one of your elderly neighbors' names right now, buy a ticket to Japan and visit a park frequented by dog owners on a Sunday afternoon. I will bet you that within twenty minutes, you will find a dog that has that name, whether it be Kurt, Frank, Ethyl or Lulu. One elderly woman erupted in laughter, in fact, when she called her golden retriever, Bob, and I answered. "You have a dog's name!" she cackled. This is similar to the chuckle you get when you tell Japanese people that there are 7-Eleven and Kentucky Fried Chicken franchises in America as well. For some reason, they seem to think that these things are Japanese in origin. Just imagine if you shouted, "Here Fido!" and a Japanese guy came running up to you. That is the situation I find myself in here, it seems.

The pet pensions feature large, fenced-in grounds that resemble American backyards. There are almost always toys for the dogs to play with. Most of the guests' free time is spent watching their dogs run around the grounds and then holding discussions similar to the one I just related. Some favorite topics: where John likes to walk; what John likes to eat; John's habits in the house; who walks John; John's bad habits; John's friends (I am not kidding. In fact, I feel like I am listening to a grade school kid back in New Jersey list off his best friends in his class).

On several occasions, people have brought their children and their pets to the pensions. Never once have I witnessed them talking about their kids. The children usually sit beside the parents looking neglected and bored. In fact, many times, they seem to be in the role we'd normally expect of the pets. (This does not mean that I have seen teenage Japanese kids roll over for dog snacks or eat out of round dishes on the floor. I'm merely implying that the dogs get far more attention than the kids do.)

Like most institutions in Japan, the pet pensions have rules: Wipe your dog's feet when you bring them into the pension; do not allow your dog to sleep on the bed, et cetera. Of course, they are not worded this way; they're more like Cold War-era East German billboards extolling communist virtues: Let's keep the dogs off the beds so that they will be clean for everyone! We want to keep the halls clean for other guests! Please feel free to use the towels at the entrance way for your dogs' paws each time you enter the pension!

But despite the rules, pet pensions are usually cozy places. Cozy and noisy. I never sleep well during my stays. All night the dogs bark to one another, communicating some sort of messages or merely making lots of racket. One of the talents of most Japanese, my wife included, is the ability to sleep through an earthquake or a major riot. I, on the other hand, lie awake all night, serenaded by a chorus of canines.

The pensions host special events, too. We once attended a Christmas party at which each dog had to do a trick or show some special talent. The two proprietors served as judges. This event was followed by a Christmas costume contest. Most of the dogs at the pensions are not only expensive, but it seems like they underwent special training. They are disciplined dogs. Boss, on the other hand, is a bit of a free spirit. This Christmas competition seemed to confirm that Boss is an outcast among dogs.

The Christmas competition featured superb performances. One dog stood on its back legs. Another barked to a song. Another jumped through hoops during a perfectly executed display of tricks. I slammed back my fourth beer with festive gusto and cheered heartily. My wife nudged me gently, and only then did I notice the disapproving glances my holiday mirth was attracting.

I dragged Boss out and announced that he would show his bilingual abilities. I then tried to make him do his litany of lame "tricks": sit, speak, shake. I quickly discovered that the program was in peril. When I told him to sit, he refused. I told him in Japanese, and he rebelled even more. I tried to shake hands with him, but he grabbed my shirt cuff and shook it violently, tail all the while wagging. I cracked up, thinking that Boss was clearly the comedy hit of the program. I looked up, however, to a sea of solemn faces. The judges bore pained expressions. To them, Boss and I were clearly rejects. We represented American entertainment interests – Boss couldn't do jack, but he could be spontaneous and funny. For this, I found him clever. To the Japanese, he was a total failure. The Japanese expect precision in public performances. Just as they expect that their child will perform *The Minute Waltz* in sixty seconds *exactly*, they demand no less of their pets. No innovation, no goofing around. If they are unable to do it well, they should not be in front of an audience (which is clearly what they were thinking about Boss and me). They were embarrassed for me, which was touching, but I found Boss' lack of talent and focus refreshing and highly entertaining. As we exited the "stage," he was yanking at my pant legs. The expressions remained melancholic, bordering on morose. Boss and I were ruining their show!

The costume contest went little better. Each animal had an expensive, handsome costume that it strutted around in. My wife had bought this cheap, exceedingly large Santa suit (ideal for someone with a pet wildebeest) and sloppily draped it over Boss. He immediately tossed it off and shook it about in his mouth. I watched proudly, largely because I thought that this contest was the most ridiculous thing I had ever witnessed in my life. Don't get me wrong: The idea was fine; the fact that people took it so seriously made it absurd. Clearly, they either needed to relax more, or hit the booze harder. I was doing both, so I was doubled over as Boss wrestled with his costume beneath the limelight, as if combating an invisible pro wrestling foe.

On this particular trip, I had brought one of our cats with us, too, as I decided to put the name "pet pension" to its ultimate test. (She was allowed to come only if we pledged that she would not "attack" any of the dogs. I was a bit puzzled and worried that the proprietor had no reciprocal pledge of safety for my cat.) Fortunately, Goldie does not mind being among dogs, and most of these dogs seemed to like this pretty, petite white cat. Even in the dining room, she allowed dogs to sniff her all over and held to the agreement by not gouging out any eyes.

In the costume contest, however, Goldie, as if following Boss' lead, ditched her costume and headed for a corner of the

room. I beamed as she joined her brother in this nonconform-
ist mutiny.

We came in last. The winners were two dogs dressed
in sharp, matching elf costumes. That they had gone to such
lengths deserves respect. I clapped enthusiastically in the corner in my natty red holiday shirt, holding Boss' and Goldie's
crumpled costumes and continuing to imbibe to augment the
enjoyment of a thorough trouncing at this odd yuletide event
in a primarily Buddhist country. (Check out the glossary entry
on Christmas in Japan for more holiday hilarity).

Later, just for fun, I asked the owner in the most earnest
voice I could muster whether the scores had been close. Dip-
lomatically, he claimed that it had been difficult to judge both
contests and then added that there had been a third activity
that we had not shown up in time for. I shot my wife a quick
glance; it was met by a shrug, which meant either "I didn't
know about it!" or "Who the hell cares?" Japanese body language consists mainly of looking expressionless, so you lose
your ability to read signs.

In any case, I pledged to try harder next year; I thought I
saw a flicker of alarm in his eye: "This guy's coming BACK????"

The end of a stay at a pet pension is by far the most awkward part. People begin to bid one another farewell. Ninety-
nine percent of the time, you have exchanged your dogs'
names, but not your own, so the only option open in Japanese
is something like this:

Table One Guy:	*(Looking at Boss, but then quickly shifting his gaze to me)* Uh … Boss, goodbye!
Me:	*(Bowing)* John, nice meeting you. *(Table One Guy bows.)*
Table One Guy:	*(Bowing again)* It was very nice get-ting acquainted. *(The word "you" is not usually used in Japan when ad-*

	dressing someone directly. Sound confusing? Somehow, it all makes sense … sort of …).
Me:	*(Bowing again)* I hope we meet again. I hope I see John again.
Table One Guy:	*(Bowing more)* John enjoyed meeting Boss.
Me:	Boss enjoyed meeting John.
Table One Guy:	I'll be rude, excuse me! *(Bows again)*
Me:	I'm being rude. You must be tired! *(Bowing)*
Table One Guy:	You must be tired, too. Uh, um, hey, uh, let's meet again, excuse me! *(Nervous bowing, walking backwards, cannot wait to get away)*
Me:	See you again. Excuse me. *(Bowing; I'm getting a little dizzy and my abdominal muscles have begun to hurt. I wish the guy would get out of here, but I do not dare convey that.)*
	(More clumsy bowing, robotic gesticulating and jerky nodding, as if someone had lit the soles of our feet or the seats of our pants on fire … the typical stuff of Japanese partings with people you really do not know, but with whom you have to be very polite.)

Repeating these awkward farewells several times, I am exhausted and relieved as we leave the pet pension. But we'll be back. And perhaps next year, the judges will loosen up a bit and see Boss for the comic genius that he is. Maybe we can spruce up his costume, and I can cut down on the brews so that I'm not too drunk for the awards ceremony. And maybe

Goldie can get into the act. That might be unique. At the very least, it might help us stay out of last place.

Above all, I'll make some new friends, even if they are dogs … as for the humans, well, we were already friends by Japanese standards, weren't we?

THAT FLOATING FEELING III
sumie kawakami
translation by yuko enomoto

Yukiko Makioka is a forty-two-year-old language school
instructor. She was interviewed in May 2003.

M Y HUSBAND IS COMING home tonight. Shall I cook
       sukiyaki? Or broil some fish in aluminum foil? The
       children might not like that. Perhaps we will have
hamburger steaks tonight and then stuff the leftover beef into
green peppers for tomorrow's lunch.

I had no work today, so I took it a little easy and went
shopping in the less crowded hours of the afternoon. Normally,
I run into the supermarket on my way home from work, fill the
shopping basket with necessities and rush home on my bicycle.
On days that I can shop leisurely like this, I buy in bulk. Frozen
foods were discounted by twenty percent today, so I bought
a few. As my mind wandered toward my children – who will
probably make a face and say, "Frozen? Again?" – I caught a
glimpse of myself in a mirror on the side of a small street.

I was wearing boot-cut pants and no makeup, a cardigan
and carrying a shopping basket. From any angle, I am an ordi-
nary-looking mom.

I'm not too frumpy for my age. I show some assertiveness in my choice of pants, wearing ones from The Gap rather
than Uniqlo. But I am not proud of the way I look. That's why
I can't believe this outrageous thing that I, a normal-looking
person, am doing. It feels like it's happening to someone else.

I never really had that much confidence in myself as a
woman. I don't have a great figure; my looks are average. I'm
not talented at any one thing, like tea ceremony, flower arrangement or dancing. I'm still a novice at work, just starting
out at this age.

So, when someone appears before me and tells me he
likes me, truth is, my initial reaction is to say, "What? Why
me?" If he becomes a little more aggressive, I'll feel high ("He
noticed me!") and before long, I become self-conscious.

At any rate, a woman my age may be more vulnerable

to such moves. This could be the last love of her life. So far, I haven't experienced the symptoms, but they say women past forty are on a steep, downward slope. And if I were to ask myself, "Where will I ever meet another man?" I feel I may never have a chance like this again. I guess that attitude is reflected in my actions. I can't help it if people think I'm loose.

"Is the fact that I flirt with practically any man connected to my lack of self-confidence?" I once asked a close friend.

She replied, "You have a lot of nerve saying that. Do you realize that for someone who lacks self-confidence, you attract an awful lot of men?"

I don't consider myself aggressive at all, but come to think of it, I sometimes think I am predisposed to romantic relationships. I seem to reel in these men.

I recently broke up with Yamamura, and he blamed me for starting it all in the first place. "It's all your fault," he said. "You seduced me." He was getting very agitated, and he screamed at me: "How are you going to take responsibility for all this?" I was just perplexed. I don't report directly to Yamamura, but he was a superior, so I was just being friendly to him in a noncommittal way, just like I treated everybody else. Imagine my surprise when he said, "That sort of nonchalance drives men crazy."

But this relationship was the worst. Yamamura was mentally unstable and towards the end, he was practically stalking me. He would be hiding in the dark, waiting for me to come home from work at night. On bad nights, he would ring the doorbell, and I would see him on the monitor standing in front of the house. Somehow, I managed to calm him down and send him home, but there were times when I broke into a cold sweat, wondering what to do in the presence of my family.

My tryst with Yamamura was a two-sided affair. He was five years younger and had two small children. Hence, we promised each other that this relationship would be based on good sense. But as soon as we began discussing our breakup, he started acting strange.

It was an office romance, so things got very complicated. Of course, I never told anybody in the office about my relationship with Yamamura, but he would almost flaunt it, acting in such obvious ways. For example, if we happen to pass each other, he would push me into the lounge and shout, "I love you so much. Why are you breaking up with me?" Then, after all that shouting, he would try to kiss me. I was scared that he was going to hurt me, so instead of fighting him off, I just froze. In fact, a few times he has pulled my hair and hit me. The fear that he would turn violent again and that everyone in the office and, in the end, my family would find out filled me with an anxiety so intense it was ripping my heart to shreds. The best I could do at times like these was to calm this angry man down and walk out of the place in one piece.

I was wrong to drag out our relationship because of fear, but in hindsight it was a mutually dependent relationship, something akin to domestic violence. When we were alone together, Yamamura would be unbelievably kind. "I'm crazy about you, Yukiko," he would say, or "I want to be with you always," he would whisper and hold me tight. I would almost blush at the thought of how much he loved me.

We each had a family, so our dates were limited in time and place. That limitation was what made it so beautiful, or should I say, within that time frame he would be very gentle with everything he did, including sex. He was like a different person.

But then, some little thing would upset him and trigger a huge mood swing, and he would be back to yelling and raging, "You've ruined my life!" Not a hint of the social graces the man demonstrates at the office. After striking me, he would fall on his knees and beg forgiveness through tears. "What have I done? Please forgive me!" He would punch his own face while saying, "It's all my fault that it turned out like this." One time, he even burned a cigarette into his hand. I feel fear and pity when I see Yamamura act like this. I start thinking, "Perhaps I'm in the wrong here for talking about breaking up," or "I wonder if he will stay calm as long as I don't break up with him." Worse yet, maybe all this really is my fault. All these thoughts kept going round and round in circles in my head, and I had trouble finding a way out of this relationship. Before I knew it, a year had gone by.

I was going neurotic at the time, seriously blaming myself for all this. (This is punishment for the adultery I had committed, I thought.) Noticing how emaciated I had become over this, a good friend from work advised me to hand in my resignation right away and get out. She would cover for me tomorrow, she said. Not once had I told her anything about my affair, but it must have been obvious. Either way, I had to resign, with Yamamura being in a senior position.

Upon learning of my resignation, Yamamura said in front of everybody, "It'll be very lonely with Yukiko quitting. I can't stop her because she won't listen to me. Will everyone try to persuade her to stay?" Such pretentiousness. Look at the way he acted when he was alone with me. For the first time, I realized that he cared only about himself. It was as if I had seen his true colors. Even after I quit work, he used to hassle me a lot. But then I'd changed my cellphone number and email, and at some point he stopped trying to contact me.

During that time, even my sons showed concern over my instability at home. "Mom, are you sick? Shouldn't you go see a doctor?" one of them would say. But when the older one asked, "Did something happen at work?" the younger one would interject, "You don't have to answer if you don't want to, mom." They must've intuited that I was trying to hide something from them.

When I told my husband that I wanted to quit work because of problems, he didn't ask why. I lightly dismissed it by telling him that I was being bullied at work. My husband didn't ask anything more. He just said, "It must've been very difficult for you." Whether that was out of good sense or complete dis-interest, I don't know.

To tell you the truth, I cried alone for a few hours this morning after my husband left for work. I was cleaning and I became sad all of a sudden.

A few years back when we decided to build our own home, my husband's one condition was to have a room he could call his own. He calls it his study, but in the end, he has moved his bed in there. He practically lives in there; he only comes out for meals. For him, the study is his castle, and he doesn't seem to want me in there. Of course, I don't feel like going in there and rummaging through his desk (for one thing, the drawers are locked). He can have his privacy. Still, I feel bad about not cleaning up, so once in a while I go in there and vacuum or make the bed.

One time, there was an open book on the bed, so I returned it to the bookshelf. His face made it clear that he didn't want me to interfere. "Don't touch my books," he said. If he would only just say, "Please don't clean the study," I would never set foot in that room. But he won't. He thinks that saying so will either be the end of us, or maybe he just wants me to clean the room. Anyway, as long as he doesn't tell me to keep out, it would be awkward and strange for me to clean all but his room. So I end up going in there for a quick vacuum and to make the bed. The end.

When you open the door ever so quietly to my husband's study, although it's in the same house, the air in that room is different. It smells of him and the pile of books. Every time I open the door, I face the plain reality that my husband lives in a place I am not allowed to enter. This distance may never narrow for as long as we're together. That thought was too much for me to take this morning. I threw down the vacuum cleaner, ran upstairs to my bed and cried.

My husband is what you'd call a perfect person. He makes a lot of money; he's very dependable. He will do anything briskly – house chores, taking care of the children. When we bought the house, he took care of the down payment and mortgage loan application all by himself. And yet, he never made any fuss about the layout or interior. I didn't even ask for it, but he gave me the ownership rights to a percentage of the house. He is usually very busy and hardly at home even on weekends, but on summer and winter vacations, we take family trips, and once we're there, he's committed to the children.

He's smart, popular at work, and he is the type of person who steadily and surely climbs the corporate ladder. He would never dispense flattery or lie just to get to the top. If he believes that something is wrong, regardless of whom he is addressing, he can speak his mind. He is a straight man and because of that, he has resigned from a job in the past. But because of his sincerity, somebody always helps him out. His popularity is commensurate with his abilities. The next work he finds is always better than the last, more worth doing. Anyway, he is extremely positive and self-confident.

He's not one of those men who think that women should stay at home. He's more understanding than the average man about my work. Truth is, I was an ordinary housewife three years ago. We lived in company-sponsored housing, where I cleaned, did the laundry, went shopping at supermarkets and sometimes went out for tea with other mothers in the neighborhood. One day would melt into the next. My husband was well paid, so we never struggled. But as my sons grew up, I began to feel anxious about just getting old with nothing to show for it.

I've thought about working – not short-term like at a supermarket, but work I can do for a long time, a profession. But that's easier said than done. When I was small, I grew up in America due to my father's business. At university, I studied English literature, and after that, my husband's work took us to America, where we lived for a short time. So language is supposed to be my strength. But life as a normal housewife has left my language skills rusty. I worried that I would completely forget English. I was also hoping that I would be able to work with small children or students, so I consulted my husband about going to school to become a language instructor.

He supported me, saying that in this day and age, a woman has to have some kind of work. He even applied to the school for me and told me not to worry about registration and tuition fees because he would take care of them. After going to school for a while, I finally landed work. He brought home some English books for me from his overseas business trips. "I thought these might help," he said.

The work schedule of a language instructor is very unstructured. It's not something I can do at my convenience, for example, while the children are at school. It often falls on weekday evenings or Saturdays. To that, my husband has said, "Work is work; a little inconvenience cannot be helped." And, if I ask him to do the household chores while I'm gone, he handles everything – the cleaning and taking care of the children – to perfection. He doesn't cook, but the boys look forward to going out to dinner with their father. They have a good time without me, just the boys hanging out together.

Even so, I feel this constant pressure, like he's looking down on me. Perhaps, in his eyes, I am at the same level as his sons: a poor woman he will take care of because she cannot stand on her own two feet. Of course, he's never said that to me directly, but his attitude tells me that he's continuing this marriage out of a sense of obligation. I fear him like a father figure, although we're only two years apart.

He was always the "I lead, you follow" type of person, even before we got married. We met at work, and that's where it all started. When he asked me out on our first date, he said, "I've called with marital intentions." I hesitated and thought to myself, "What is this?" But without even asking what he meant by that, I accepted, and we continued dating. Next thing I knew, we were making wedding plans.

Of course, there was a time when I actually was attracted to his assertiveness. When I look back on our marriage, I see that there was a time when we were a very happy married couple. Our life in America was truly happy. Both my sons were born there. Naturally, I was apprehensive about giving birth for the first time in a foreign country. But I knew everything would turn out fine because he was with me. That's how dependable he was.

We stayed in America for five years, and during those years we would hop into the car for a family trip, cook meals together … It may have something to do with the national character of that country, but it really struck me that family life could be so warm. A dependable husband, a leisurely life, beautiful children – those were happy days. Come to think of it, we were still sleeping in a double bed back then. That was only natural for us at the time.

Married life started falling apart after we returned to Japan. Work was very hard. He came home late every night and was hardly ever home on weekends. In time, we started sleeping on separate beds. Before I knew it, we were not having any sex, let alone conversation. The only words we exchange these days are, "I'm leaving," or, "Are you having dinner at home?" or, "I have to work, so I'll leave things up to you," and other administrative exchanges. That's the only way we can converse now.

We can barely communicate with each other, and our sons have to mediate between us. My older son, who is in middle school, said to me: "Mom, you always seem so timid in front of Dad. Why can't you just speak out?"

My son is becoming rebellious toward his father lately, so maybe he is merely impatient with my wishy-washy ways.

That's when my younger son – the one with the gentler disposition – would say, "Dad is strict, but he has a lot of good traits, too," and take sides with him. Just the other day, he said, "Mom is really tired. Dad said we have to take care of you."

I'm usually treated coldly, so when I hear something like that, I am moved to tears. He is not an evil man. I know that. In fact, sometimes I wonder why I am so fearful of my own husband. Perhaps I am just spoiled. Could it be because I am the youngest sister in my family? I hate being alone, and I'd rather be pulled along than lead. But I can never lean on my husband. I constantly feel like I am being reproached.

Until a few years ago, I made an effort to communicate with my husband. I even asked him, "How can I get closer to you?"

My husband has worked very hard to get to where he is now. He came from a poor family and made his way through college by delivering newspapers. He took advantage of the company's overseas study program and got his MBA, which he eventually used as a springboard to a better job. I can understand his irritation with a slow-going person like myself, living a comfortable life. When he says, "How can a person who floats through life like yourself understand what I am going through?" I have no words to reply with. I certainly am happy-go-lucky, and I probably do not grasp the harshness of my husband's corporate environment. But if he talked to me about it, even a little, I think I could understand. If I try to ask, he pushes me away, bothered by my prying.

After repeating this scenario over a number of years, I decided at some point not to bother. The desire to connect with him was simply my problem and of no interest whatsoever to my husband. It's very lonely, but it's a problem I have to solve on my own.

It was difficult at first. I originally sought a relationship out of loneliness, I think. My first infidelity was with a friend from college, right before I began working. We met at some gathering, and as we talked over the phone and dated a few times, we sort of stumbled into a relationship. He was married, so he tried to break it off by saying, "This is not good. Let's break up." To which I reluctantly agreed. But then, about six months later, we would start feeling lonely, and we saw see each other once in a while.

The next person was a student sixteen years my junior. He was my student. At first, being so much older than him, I treated him more like a son than a man. But then, as time went on, he said to me, "I am not very good at talking about myself. But with you, I can say anything. Why are you so kind to me?" At the time, I got flustered. But things kept rolling, and before I knew it, we were going to the museum, to the movies. It didn't take that long for the relationship to turn physical.

I was walking on clouds. On a Sunday afternoon, which is normally spent at home staring at the TV or vacuuming, I am walking hand in hand with a man much younger than I. More than anything else, though, the youthful energy and the seriousness with which he loved me were so refreshing. It made me happy.

We lasted only about six months. I think he was too young to accept the dishonesty. "Yuki, you are deceitful," he said to me. I had no response to that. I am, in fact, deceitful. But, at the time, it was a huge heartbreak for me. For a while, I just stayed home, stunned at what had happened. Only now do I appreciate it for what it was: a short but wonderful dream.

If you ask me whether I truly loved those men, my answer may be "no." I never once thought about divorcing my husband and being with these men.

I now find myself in a normal state after hours of crying. I have my work; I have no time to mope around. Having affairs, working – this was originally my way out of loneliness. But that doesn't mean it was all bad. There have been times when I wondered, "What on earth am I doing?" Theories aside, perhaps, things are the way they are only because I'd willed them to be so.

Except, I don't consider myself one to fall for someone that easily. Even if there is a man I have feelings for, I don't have the courage or the good looks to make the first move.

That's why, for me, relationships have always been up to the other person. He starts prodding, and the next thing I know, I've developed feelings for him. It's always been that way.

For women who are used to being told that they are beautiful from an early age, seduction is something of a daily experience. A push or two is not going to sway that sort of woman romantically. Either that or they are moved like crazy, but they're also thinking, "Oh well, I'm married, and that's not adult-like behavior, so I won't do it." They possess a grounded-ness that comes from confidence.

But if a person like myself is going around nonchalantly having a series of affairs, imagine all those people out there who may have a mountain of experience with infidelity. They're walking around with a look on their face that says, "I have class," and they're tastefully clad in brand-name clothing, not in an ostentatious way, though. Those are the kinds of people who may be having affairs left and right.

When I was coming down from my affair with Yama-mura, I was up to here with the likes of stalkers and violent types. I thought to myself, "I can't fall in love again," but I have a feeling that I might, very easily. Women are so selfish.

In fact, there is a man who has feelings for me right now. Mr. Kazama is a student where I teach, and he is ten years my senior, with a wife. After his two children went off to college, he decided that he wanted to take a trip abroad, so he came to our school to study English. He says it was love at first sight for him, but since life is long, let us first take good care of our family, all the while nurturing a long-lasting relationship.

That doesn't sound too bad. I'm in no hurry to jump into it this time. We've had a few meals together, but for the time being I have no plans to take it a step further with Mr. Kazama. And lately, I've come to realize that as long as I am married, there's no sense in letting myself fall so easily and then getting burned in a relationship that will end sooner or later. If you re-spond favorably to a person who shows interest in you, he will develop cold feet. If, on the other hand, you try to take flight, he will pursue you tenaciously. No matter how far you go in an illicit relationship, you always end up in a vicious circle. If there's no possibility for a happy ending, it's going to simply end. Saying good-bye is never easy, even when you are prepared for it. That's why I think it would be so cool to be able to say, "Let's stay friends."

For now, whether I fall in love again or not, I really want to have more self-confidence. Working has helped a little in that respect. These days I spend my own money to buy my own things, which I think is helping me become a little more independent.

But, no matter how much I run, I can never catch up with my husband. In terms of our married life, I have no expectations. I probably will never have sex with him again.

Sometimes I wonder if my husband is seeing someone else, too. Come to think of it, he did tell me several years ago that there was such a person. At the time, I, too, was seeing somebody else, so my response was a cool, "Oh, really?" It made sense to me that since I was having fun, he should be having fun, too. In hindsight, we were at least on speaking terms back then.

Whatever happened to his relationship with the woman after that conversation, I do not know. I also don't know if he's seeing someone now. If he is, I'm not surprised. When my husband leaves the house on a Sunday afternoon, I don't even ask him where he is going. I don't think I ever will.

We don't discuss divorce mainly because of the children, I think. There are no strong reasons for us to get a divorce right away. My husband is a good person, and I can continue to live with him in the manner that roommates sharing an apartment get along with each other. We'll leave each other alone, cooperate when we have to – that sort of relationship will continue at least until the children are grown up.

Of course, what could be better than living with a man

who will keep you in his warm embrace? My husband is unlikely to do so. Maybe that's why I keep running to other men. While these affairs are short, they still give me some self-esteem, let me dream. But then again, no matter how much I like them, if I live with them, I will end up in the same place. Buried under the daily chores of baths, meals and cleaning, we all end up losing a little bit of luster each day.

Mr. Kazama says to me, "Why do you lack self-confidence? For me, just talking with you is so healing. Why can't you see that?" The answer to that is, because I have yet to be recognized by my husband of more than ten years. He is my one true love. And yet, he doesn't take me in, won't even talk to me … That's why, no matter how many people say they like me, I cannot be healed.

A VERY HAPPY LIFE

takehiko kambayashi

F OR FORTY YEARS, Mie Ueda worked as a telephone operator and raised three children. Once she retired, she filled her days with luncheons and teas with friends, trips to the local gym and aqua aerobics classes. She and her husband traveled to hot springs resorts and took occasional overseas trips. They finally had the time and money to relax and enjoy themselves. This was the ideal way to pass the autumn of their lives.

Or was it?

"Sachi" woke up every day to the threat of violence. By the time she had reached her mid-fifties, she had been smacked, kicked and punched by her husband for a quarter of a century. He would twist her arms, throw her against the front door, kick her out of the house and leave her to lie there, too debilitated to move or say a word. He was so autocratic that she needed his permission to use the bathroom. Under his regime of terror, Sachi, who weighed 110 when they were married, had been reduced to an emaciated seventy-three pounds.

Sachi's husband, a local government employee who worked in the welfare division, had a good reputation at work. He often invited his colleagues home for dinner and drinks. At times, they'd surprise Sachi by showing up late at night. One time, she recalled washing more than a hundred dishes in the kitchen after putting out an array of food and drinks. Yet as soon as the guests left, Sachi's husband started punching her, yelling, "You humiliated me!"

"I was not very satisfied with my life," Mie recalls in her clear Osaka accent. "I could not help but feel emptiness. I got worried about whether I was doing the right thing. I kept asking myself, 'I didn't keep working hard just to do things like this, did I? Was my forty-year career just for dawdling my time away?'"

Mie sometimes doubts whether she and her husband were good parents. She also finds flaws in her generation's values. "Didn't we think that children were just fine as long as they got good grades at school or they got a job at a so-called good company? I have to say our generation was at fault … After all, it's how you raise a child that is important," she says.

Mie has two sons and a daughter. She says she deeply regrets that she and her husband, just like many parents of her generation, were too busy working to spare much time for their children. "That was wrong," she acknowledges.

Their two sons graduated from American universities and now work in the United States. The older son went to Arizona in his teens and toiled in cornfields while going to a local high school. She has visited the sons in the US and likes to talk about how they both take very good care of their babies and do household chores.

"If you don't respect yourself, you are less likely to treat your partner well. If you have self-esteem, you are more likely to respect your partner and others," she asserts. But instead of trying to develop their child's self-esteem, parents seem to bring up "both boys and girls so that they fit into the institution of marriage," she says. "We very often hear that someone is seen as a respectable member of society once he or she gets married."

Mie recalls being told that "patience is a virtue" when she was growing up. "In those days, this society was not mature enough for women to pursue a career," she recalls. "A woman's career was supposed to be spent as a housewife."

Mie's mother, Hamaji, turns ninety-four this year. Hamaji used to tell Mie she could find happiness by depending on her husband. But Mie's father wasn't adept at physical labor. He was probably the last person they could depend on, Mie says. She and her four brothers and three sisters led a life of misery and often had to scrape together money to get by. She describes her parents as "a poor couple with many children."

"It was unimaginable to me that I should depend on just one man for my fate. I decided to keep working no matter what," she recalls.

"Though my family was poor, I read a lot of books, trying to get as much knowledge from them as I could," she says, glancing at the dozens of books neatly aligned in her bookshelf. "I could not afford to buy them. But when I stopped by a friend's house, I very often started reading their books rather than chatting with them, which they didn't seem to like."

Upon graduating from junior high school, Mie began to work as a telephone operator while attending night school. She did this for four years. Later, she got married.

"At first my husband and I did not have anything. We started from scratch," she recalls.

A government survey completed in the year 2000 reports that 27.5 percent of wives in Japan have been beaten by their husbands. Another study found that 4.6 percent of women surveyed had been put in a life-threatening situation because of spousal abuse. Domestic violence in Japan takes the lives of more than 120 women every year, according to several private groups that deal with the issue.

Experts and activists argue that since many people still regard violence against women as a "family matter" – not a human rights issue – and that shelters for battered women are few and far between (there are only thirty private shelters in Japan), the actual number of spousal-abuse cases is probably much higher.

"Social problems like domestic violence are overlooked in this country while the so-called IT revolution and other industrial-development projects are given top priority," says Yuriko Matsuzaki, director of the Asian Women's Center, a nonprofit organization in Fukuoka that provides abused women with support, counseling and shelters.

Mie has a life-affirming demeanor despite a childhood of poverty. Today she lives a modest life with her husband, who helps out with the household chores. "When I retired, I said to him, 'I was a housewife for more than thirty years, so I cede the position to you,'" Mie says. "He seems to enjoy it. He hums while he cooks."

Mie's doubts about retirement led her to rethink her priorities. She decided to do something to help women. That's when she ran into an old acquaintance, a city council member, who told her about how domestic violence was being dealt with. "To be honest, I did not even know what *DV* even stood for," she recalls. (In Japanese, the word for domestic violence is taken from the initials of the English phrase.)

In April 1996, Mie established Space Enjo, a two-room wooden apartment that became the first shelter for battered women in Osaka, Japan's second-largest city. She spent the equivalent of several hundred dollars a month of her own money to pay the rent. Soon she was swamped with calls for help from women struggling to escape the vicious cycle of violence. Mie was inundated with horrific stories. Some women arrived at the shelter with black eyes or purplish bruises all over their bodies. Mie was shocked – this was far more serious than she had imagined. The two tiny rooms she rented were never vacant – sometimes three or four women had to be squeezed in together.

In 1998, another landlord rented more rooms to Mie at a discount. Soon battered women were arriving with their children. Mie realized that the problem cried for a more extravagant approach.

In 2001, Mie purchased a four-room condominium with a state-of-the-art security system in her neighborhood for twenty-four million yen (about two-hundred thousand dollars). She had to borrow it from her husband – each month she pays him a little bit back.

"My husband begged me to do this after he dies," she

jokes. "But I told him flatly, 'That will be too late. I need the money now.'"

Space Enjo has given refuge to more than three-hundred women and children. The victims are of diverse nationality and range in age from seventeen to seventy-eight. They were battered by their husbands, exes, parents, children, even their grandchildren.

Mie's staff of five is all volunteer and all female. All of them live off their pensions. Space Enjo uses donations to scrape by. The staff helps victims meet lawyers, real-estate agents, government employees and others who will help them rebuild their lives.

Mie's luxurious but empty retirement has given way to an active, sometimes angry one. She joined a group of activists, lawyers and victims of domestic violence calling on the government to acknowledge the *DV* crisis. In 2001, the Diet passed a law allowing victims to request restraining orders. While critics say it's far too little to combat the violence waged against women in the home, Mie says the ability to file for a restraining order means a lot to battered spouses trying to rebuild their lives.

In some cases, she says, victims have suffered from a "full course" of domestic violence, in which the husband afflicts physical, psychological and economic damage on the wife. "I'm always irritated. Why in the world does he have to hit her?" she says. "If he were in front of me, I would shout at him, 'You beast! Go to hell!'"

She's also angered at family members who try to rush victims into new marriages once the old, abusive one has ended. "They are fed up with married life and want to ease their pain. But some parents still pressure them to remarry, saying 'If you are still in your thirties, you are more likely to get a good marriage offer. But if you are in your forties or fifties, it's too late to be able to have a happy life,'" Mie says as she rolls her eyes.

Victims of abuse often think that some of the fault must be theirs. "They are excessively patient," Mie contends. "The first thing I tell a battered woman is 'It's not you who is wrong.'"

It's not you who is wrong. Those are the words Sachi heard when she checked into Space Enjo to end her violence-ridden marriage. Mie says it was one of the worst cases of abuse she has ever seen. "For twenty-five years! She put up with such a husband for twenty-five years! And she even served his guests a full-course Japanese dinner like some sort of high-class restaurant," she says with rising indignation. "In all the wide world, Japan is the only country where you would see such a case."

Sachi wanted to die when she arrived, Mie says. But today, the sixty-year-old woman lives on her own and goes to night school. She studies calligraphy. Mie holds up a work of calligraphy that Sachi has sent. "Very beautiful, isn't it? I'm going to put it in a frame and hang it on the wall here. I'm extremely pleased."

Twenty percent of the women at Space Enjo leave without saying a word, Mie estimates. Others thank the staff for the second chance. "They've taught me a lot about the world," she says emphatically. "They are resilient, tenacious and courageous."

Does she have any regrets?

"No," she says promptly and then mulls the question for a while. "What I have gained through my activity has enriched my life. Even if I could spend the rest of my life traveling as much as I want, I would never be able to grasp this richness. I never imagined I could have a very happy life like this in my sixties."

LUNCH BREAK
david cady

A PRIL FIFTEENTH, 2003. Time for lunch. ◆ Leave office at 1:05 PM. ◆ Arrive at Chiyoda Ward gym at 1:09. ◆ Change clothes, begin workout at 1:14. ◆ Stretch for three minutes. ◆ Bench: 10 reps x 55kg, 5 x 65, 2 x 75, 5 x 80, 4 x 75, 6 x 70, 7 x 65 ◆ Incline dumbbell press: 10 x 25, 8 x 25, 7 x 27.5 ◆ Lat pulldowns: 10 x 69.5, 8+1 x 74.5, 7+3 x 69.5 ◆ Saws: 10 x 22.5, 10 x 22.5, 8 x 25 ◆ Chin-ups (wide grip): 8, 5, 3 ◆ Check weight: 76.8kg ◆ Return to locker room at 1:55. ◆ Wash hands, face, towel off – no time for shower – spray pits, back, crotch with Gatsby Ice Type deodorant spray. ◆ Check stupid Jim Carrey ala *Dumb and Dumber* hair in mirror. ◆ Leave gym at 2:05. ◆ Say "*dohmo!*" to staff at front desk on way out. Have fleeting paranoid thought that they think I'm gay. Make sure wedding band is visible when waving hand. Trace gay paranoia to time when Michael, graphic designer at same company, calls me a fag for working out instead of going to lunch with him. ◆ Already late, so hustle across street to 7-Eleven to pick up lunch. ◆ Buy pickled plum rice ball, fermented soybean rice/seaweed wrap, cup of yogurt, green mixed salad with broccoli and asparagus, string cheese, Perfect Plus "multibalance nutritional food bar," two packs of soy milk. ◆ Return to office, show ID to surly racist guard at front entrance. The man literally refuses to acknowledge foreigners. Several earnest attempts to get the asshole to address me have ended in failure. He showers *ohayos* on employees as they stream in to work every morning, but as soon as he sees a foreigner, the bastard clams up. He won't even address Michael, who's Chinese-English. ◆ Take elevator up to fifth floor, reach desk at 2:15. ◆ Begin editing story titled "Versatile electronic dictionaries catching heart of wide-ranging consumers." ◆ Realize I have dead-end media job that tries to pass off corporate PR as news. ◆ Begin daydreaming about me somehow being every member of Radiohead simultaneously and giving concert in my high school gym. The audience – my peers – is visibly moved by my virtuosic musical abilities and tremendous depth of soul, which they had once so stupidly overlooked. All are reduced to tears. I forgive them. Despite my mighty powers, I choose to be benevolent. ◆ Shaken from reverie by phone call. A man of possibly Indian extraction judging from his rich brogue informs me that he has an "exciting investment opportunity" to share with me. I ask him how he got my name. He says, "From someone." I say, "Thanks, bye."

WORK
bruce rutledge

B Y THE END OF MY DOT-COM SUMMER, I was chain
smoking and drinking during the day. I felt like a war
correspondent in some godforsaken corner of the New
Economy. I started the summer of 2000 with a dream of creating an online news service in Japan, and I ended it – forty-sev-
en days later – with a hacker's cough, a new lawyer and a plane
ticket to Cleveland.

My dot-com summer was spent with a marketing manager who slept on his friend's kitchen floor; a lanky, constantly
wired Canadian whose business card read "Evangelist"; and
a Glaswegian CEO who could often be seen playing with his
Booska doll or staring at i-mode sites on his cellphone. My task
as managing editor of this dot-com was to build the most popular news portal in Japan in six short months.

But the story starts well before my adventure. In 1994,
my future boss and his wife – I'll call them Mike and Mindy
McEwan – sat with their lawyer in a meeting room in the headquarters of the *Yomiuri Shimbun*, the world's largest newspaper.
The McEwans were producing a sheet of classified ads, which
the English-language *Daily Yomiuri* newspaper distributed as
an insert, but the paper had decided that the insert would have
to go.

Stephen Simms of the *Daily Yomiuri*'s circulation department recalled the meeting with Mike, who goes by the name
"Sparky." "I didn't know Spanky from boo," Simms said, inten-
tionally botching Mike's nickname. "I was just trying to help
him out. But we just couldn't have ads for dogs having sex with
cats and open-minded couples looking for sexual encounters.
The *Yomiuri* is a family newspaper."

Simms told the McEwans and their lawyer that he had
warned them about their ad content, and the Yomiuri would
no longer carry their insert. Mike vehemently denied being
warned, called Simms a "fucking liar" and demanded his First
Amendment rights.

Simms, flanked by two Japanese employees, told Mike

that Japan had no First Amendment. "This isn't the US," he reminded the livid CEO.

¶ The McEwans could be seen after that passing out their page of classifieds to foreigners on Tokyo street corners. They were not about to let the Yomiuri crush them.

About six years later, they ran a company I'll call Crossroads. Their staff of about twenty produced a weekly magazine. Mindy had been the CEO in the early days, but now Mike was in charge. Their free magazine had sixty pages, a circulation of close to forty-thousand and a slew of classified ads. Take that Yomiuri!

But the McEwans had even grander ideas. In the spring of 2000, I was shown a business plan that made me think it was time to change jobs. The vision was bold – a website that would produce daily news about Japan in Japanese and English. The McEwans were ambitious. They threw huge parties at the Velfarre disco in Tokyo's Roppongi nightclub district, lived in a very expensive apartment just off the city's most fashionable street, Omote Sando, and led a staff that looked like it had just returned from a night of raving to produce, each week, a slick-looking magazine. Perhaps, just perhaps, they could actually build a respectable online news source, I thought.

My introduction to the McEwans came through the Evangelist. In a taxi after a late-night shift of editing at a business newspaper where I was in charge of the copy editing, he told me about a project his friends were launching with seven million dollars in startup funds. They were looking for a managing editor, and he wondered if I knew anyone. "Of course," he said as we pulled up to his apartment building, "I would really like to introduce you; but you're pretty set, aren't you?"

He had successfully planted the seed. Two days later, I discussed the project with Yuko, my wife. Soon we were pondering just what sort of offer I would need to let go of the health insurance, pension and $120,000-a-year salary of my current post.

While I had a stable job, I also worked for an extremely old-school company. On one of my first days, I was called to the personnel department to sign my contract and go over some details. One detail included the option of having two monthly salary payments. You could send eighty or ninety percent of your salary to the joint account you held with your wife, the personnel manager explained with a big grin, then send the rest to a secret account. Sweet!

But then the personnel manager placed a small sheet of paper in front of me which explained that for the first six months, I would be allowed " minus one" vacation days. It was right there in front of me in black and white: -1. I jokingly asked which Sunday they would like me to work, thinking it was a mistake. It was not. I was being hired as a full-time employee, they explained, while almost all the other foreigners were hired as independent contractors, paid hourly wages and offered little or no benefits. Since employees of this newspaper regularly put in six-day workweeks and I only worked five days a week, they adjusted my vacation days accordingly.

Back in the newsroom, my boss told me I could take ten vacation days a year, and he would cover for me by pretending I was working those days. Still, I couldn't shake the lingering desire to blow something up.

After several years at this paper, I was desperate for an adventure. Yuko and I agreed that I should take the dot-com job even if it meant a pay cut. We set a floor of eleven million yen, or about $110,000, plus stock options. On May second, the thirty-four-year-old Mike "Sparky" McEwan offered me fifteen million yen and stock options to become managing editor of the online news service with full editorial control. I signed immediately.

A few weeks later at my *sayonara* party, I was asked to say a few words. I told the staff how much I would miss them, that I really enjoyed my time with them and how I hoped they would continue to put out a good newspaper each week. A Japanese editorial writer interrupted me. "How many stock options did you get?" The staff burst out laughing.

¶ On May twenty-second, I met Robert Jefferson, a tall, elegant black man from Bloomberg TV. He told me as we had a beer at a Mexican restaurant near the Crossroads office that he had literally memorized parts of the business plan. Jefferson, almost forty at the time, began his professional radio career when he was sixteen. His voice boomed with authority as he talked about why he was willing to leave Bloomberg to take a chance on this dot-com. I decided to hire him in about thirty minutes.

¶ On May thirtieth, my daughter played with her friends near a tree in a Tokyo park. A swarm of large crows swooped down and one scratched Kimiko on the head, drawing blood. Yuko rushed Kimiko to the hospital to get the cuts treated. That night, about twelve hours before I started my new job, Kimiko asked me to close the windows before she went to bed. She looked at me, wide-eyed, and asked, "Birds gonna eat me?"

¶ At work, things went slow at first. Robert and I didn't have desks or computers for a few days. It's a dot-com thing, we told each other. We'd just have to be patient. We didn't have a place to hang our jackets, so we stopped wearing them. Robert let his beard grow. And for a couple of days we shared an old Macintosh computer with a front panel that kept falling off. Dot-com, we said, dot-com.

We were soon flooded with resumes in response to one help-wanted ad we placed in *The Japan Times*. Inquiries had come from just about all of Japan's major media outlets. This

was the country of jobs for life? Evidently, the Japanese were either bored with the status quo or just as hungry for riches and
excitement as we were.

Those we interviewed looked stunned, impressed or be-
mused as they sat across the table from an African American
from Penllyn, Pennsylvania, and a blonde-haired, blue-eyed
man from Cleveland, Ohio, both speaking Japanese.

"I felt that there was hope for journalism in Japan," Jefferson said about those days spent interviewing. "I saw the spark
in their eyes, the vibrancy. They were willing to do it with us
– foreigners!"

But for several weeks, before we signed our first Japanese
employee, a reporter from Bloomberg, we were just a bunch of
foreigners with high hopes. We were supposed to build a bilingual news site in Japan, yet we had no Japanese staff. This troubled me. Mike rejected one of our proposed hires – a young
Japanese translator who had been living in Paris – because he
spoke English haltingly. "If they aren't bilingual, I don't want to
know them," he said. We argued that it was *us* who needed to
be bilingual, not the Japanese staff. But he refused to budge.

Other worrisome signs emerged. I found that Mindy had
once fired Mike. I also heard tales of Mike leaping over a table
to punch one of his employees. Hmmm. And for some reason,
Mike rarely carried his cellphone with him when he went out;
it would sit on his desk, writhing to "Sweet Child O' Mine" by
Guns N' Roses every time someone called him.

Mike had several meetings with an interior decorator I'll
call Billy Bronze. We were moving into a posh office in a high-
rise near Shibuya Station, and Mike had grand designs for the
space. There would be a broadcast studio, a glassed in office
for the CEO, a staff of ninety or so spread across the space, a
kitchenette and a couple of private meeting areas. A reception-
ist would greet visitors, and the front entrance would borrow
a style from a trendy Omote Sando boutique that had a bluish
translucent exterior punctuated by dark blue polka dots.

The McEwans held a daylong branding session and came up with this motto for the site: "My fresh and friendly national newspaper." I made a mental note to press the delete key violently if those words ever appeared on the site in that particular order.

And then this: There was no seven million dollars; not even the one-and-a-half million dollars we had been told would soon be in the bank. Mike said we had about a half million dollars from angel investors, but more would be coming soon. Hmmm.

¶ At the office, we were being filmed by two teachers from Temple University's Japan campus. They were promised access to our meetings in the spirit of open media. It seemed like a good idea at the time, but later the continual presence of cameras started to grate on us.

At one meeting, our executive producer – a man who had been hired from a major Western news agency to help us create a real, high-tech, twenty-four-hour newsroom – fell asleep as the camera whirred. The producer was going through family problems – an illness at home, a marriage that was on the rocks – but the cameras didn't capture that. The producer kept nodding off, waking up and interjecting comments while half asleep.

One day while Robert and I were on the balcony talking, a commotion began in a corner of the office we were sharing with the Crossroads staff. "How dare you! How dare you just say you're resigning without thanking us for everything we did for you!" Mike had exploded, his voice almost breaking as it rose in a heavy Glaswegian brogue toward new heights of indignation. "How dare you!"

Before we knew what was happening, Aeve Baldwin, managing editor of the weekly magazine, was being led to the door by Mindy. That was the end of Aeve's three-year tenure.

Aeve recalled the moment: "I did not cry, I did not laugh. I was in mild shock coupled with mild embarrassment at the way I was so graciously escorted to the door by Mindy … I spent the next two days in bed watching TV and answering the phone, which pretty much didn't stop ringing."

It seems that the problems began when Aeve and several others refused to pitch in for a bouquet of flowers for Mindy's birthday. Mindy told me later that "it was about respect. I mean, we brought her up from being a typist." Aeve did start as a typist at Crossroads, but she was also a graduate of Brooklyn Law School.

¶ The following day, the site's systems engineer (I'll call him Rex Feral, per his request) sat surrounded by computers and other equipment. Rex had begun to make Robert nervous because he often wore army fatigues, had a shaved head and impressive mutton-chop sideburns, giving him the look of a member of the Michigan militia. Rex would often disappear behind a stack of computers in the back of the room and stay there for hours, reading or listening to his Walkman. This made Robert wonder just what Rex thought of black people. (What Robert didn't realize was that Rex had a sweet tooth, often asked friends out for cake at one of his favorite patisseries and loved kittens.) On this particular day, though, Rex was approached by Mike, who was wearing his favorite grey suit. "May I have a word with you in my office?" The engineer's mind raced. What had he done? Would his friendship with Aeve do him in? He needed a work visa and was just weeks away from getting it.

Inside Mike's office, the balding CEO looked across his desk at the engineer. "When I ask you to do something, I expect it to get done," he said. The engineer braced himself for the worst. Last night, Mike said, he noticed that the engineer had left his computer monitor on. Hadn't they told him that all monitors must be turned off before employees go home?

The engineer later reflected: "I mean there are cheap Scots, and there are *cheap Scots* … "

¶ A few days later, Mike called me into his office. "May I have a word with you?" He told me the producer had missed an important meeting with a potential investor and asked me if I would mind if he were let go. "You mean you're firing him?" I asked. Mike nodded. Did I mind? Sure I minded, I thought. I minded that Mike messed with people's lives, hiring them, then discarding them like so much rubbish. I minded that he was constantly looking for excuses to demean his staff. I minded that he obviously had no need for a "producer," but he hired one anyway. I looked Mike in the eye and said, no, I didn't have a problem with it. Go ahead and fire him.

The producer begged to keep his job. He said it would end his marriage if he were fired. Mike offered to let him resign, but the producer wouldn't. He believed in the project. Please, please, please.

The producer's dot-com summer lasted about a week. "Kiss Mike's ass for as long as you can," was his parting advice to me.

Meanwhile, my staff grew. We hired three people from Bloomberg, an Australian freelancer, a multilingual Yugoslavian woman, a Japanese environmental reporter and a copy editor from the *Nikkei Shimbun* whose wife was pregnant with their first child.

Robert and I learned website layout from the weekly magazine's web designer, a young redhead named Kate with a tattoo and a pierced lip. Kate, recently engaged, had been working late hours with no extra pay to help us get the site ready. Mike told me to make sure she had a front-page template up by a certain date. That date came and went.

One afternoon Mike told the marketing director that we needed a "pep talk." His idea of a pep talk was to berate me in front of the staff for not holding Kate to her deadline. Robert seemed to almost rise out of his chair with indignation as Mike lectured about respecting deadlines. I said that if Mike really wanted the front-page template up quickly I could hire free-lancers who we could pay to do it. Mindy asked Mike, "What's wrong with that?" Mike's voice rose an octave. "It will just be the same," he said inexplicably. By the end of the meeting, he vowed to do the template himself. I ranted to my staff and any-one else who cared to listen about how I thought Mike's tactics were bush league. Finally Mindy approached to calm things down. She told me in soothing tones that she and Mike were just used to doing things themselves and sometimes they got frustrated with their employees. When they first started Cross-roads, she said, they didn't even know how to buy a desk in Ja-pan. But instead of letting that stop them, she explained, they built their own.

¶ On the thirty-seventh day of my dot-com summer, I asked Mike if I could redo the front page of the site, which at this point announced the coming of the online news site as if it were a new clothing line, saying that it would be "hip" and "cool." He said yes. I wrote a brief introduction of our proj-ect that mentioned "an unlikely band of professionals" leaving "respectable media organizations" to launch a news service. I wrote that the editorial team was rubbing shoulders with the weekly magazine staff with their piercings and tattoos, and that we were leaving our suits and ties at home and getting ready for an exciting journey. The editorial team loved it. The McE-wans did not.

The following Monday, Mike told me to change the text. I decided silently that I wouldn't. Here was my chance to test him. Was I really in charge of the editorial content, as had been promised? If so, he was suggesting a change, not demanding one. And to show my dot-com spirit, I even wrote him an alternative that was more businesslike. If he liked it, I would be glad to put it up.

Days went by. On July fourteenth, the forty-fourth day of my dot-com summer, we moved into our new office. The McEwans had hired one man, Eddie, to move the entire office. Robert, me and a Canadian journalist who was in the fifth day of his dot-com summer helped. Rex, who had secured his work visa, steadfastly refused to lift a finger. The marketing director told Rex ominously, "That's gonna come back to haunt you, man."

As we helped Eddie lift chairs and desks on this sweltering July day, Mike and the marketing director had a meeting at the new office with Billy Bronze. Mike was wearing his favorite grey suit.

Around five in the afternoon my cellphone rang. It was the copy editor at the *Nikkei* who would be joining our team in little over a week. He asked what had happened to the front page of the website.

"What do you mean?"

"The writing's been changed."

Mike had reduced my text to a few innocuous lines about an online news site coming soon. I knew that, journalistically speaking, the text wasn't really worth going to the wall for. After all, it was a PR piece. But something in me snapped.

I called Mike's cellphone and left an angry message. I cursed Mike's name in front of the staff. I sent Mike an angry email demanding a meeting with him and my staff. That weekend, Mindy and the marketing director called me several times. I let them talk to the answering machine. Meanwhile, I found myself a new lawyer and began calling travel agents to see if there was still time to book a flight to Cleveland to visit my parents. On Monday, I dressed in black.

Mike fired me over the cellphone while I was eating a lunch of raw fish and rice. The three senior editors on my team persuaded me to meet Mike and Mindy one last time that evening. The meeting lasted two hours. We agreed on almost nothing. Mike told me there were three points he wanted to make: I had to respect the company's schedule, I had to produce more content, and – "What was the other one, Mindy?" – oh yeah, I had accumulated too much power. Mindy said I "mystified" them. I had been on the job seven weeks and what had I produced? At the end of the meeting, Mindy said, "Can we at least agree that in this company the publisher will be involved in the editorial process?" I looked at Mindy and said, "No." My forty-seventh day had come to a close.

The following morning, Mike offered the Canadian editor my job. He quit on the spot. The day after that, Robert approached Mike. "I want my life back," Robert said. His dot-com summer ended that day.

Should I have challenged Mike over a piece of PR puffery when the larger battle of building an online news service remained to be fought? Maybe not. But in the end, I realized, dot-com or not, something fundamental was at stake.

I came out of that final meeting feeling almost high. I was the McEwan's Good Soldier Svejk. I had "mystified" them. That, to me, was priceless.

TOKUDAIJI DAYS
wil fennell

ZEN COWBOY

"I FEEL CLOSE TO GOD when I'm good and drunk." Gerald Hogan was raising another cup of Mountain Mist sake to his lips as he spoke the words. He took it down in a silent gulp and let out a bellowing "Oof!"

Close to God. This brand of near-nonsense would have been laughable coming from anyone else, but Gerald was a professional, after all, with the resonant voice, the assured manner and the sheer presence to make these pronouncements stick.

I poured another cup for the three of us – Gerald, my friend Mike and myself – and as we raised our cups, instead of the usual "cheers," Mike quipped, "Nearer my God to thee, eh Gerald?"

"Exactly. That's the ticket, boys," Gerald said with a grin. Then it was down the hatch and another "Oof!"

My first image of Gerald Hogan had come during a phone call just after Mike moved into Tokudaiji, a worn and weary but enchanted Buddhist temple located in the country-side of Kyoto prefecture. Mike mentioned that his new neighbor was an eccentric Buddhist priest from Oklahoma, and into my mind drifted the figure of a lanky young ranch hand in a ten-gallon Stetson and snakeskin boots. Wrap him in a kimono instead of Levi's and leather chaps, and replace his six shooter with a samurai sword, and voila – the Zen Cowboy.

"How old is this guy?" I asked Mike.

"Ancient," he said, and in that split second the Zen Cowboy image vanished from my mind.

Mike was the temporary caretaker of Tokudaiji, and I visited him often during his summer there. The temple was situated among thick evergreens at the top of a long and steep cobblestone path. On those occasions when I arrived alone at the bottom of those steps, the phrase "the middle of nowhere" ran through my head in spite of my resistance to the cliché.

Once, as I made a slow climb up the path, I played around with the word "nowhere" the way E. E. Cummings does in one of his poems: Nowhere. Now. Here.

The first time I met Gerald, he was sitting cross-legged on the tatami in the main room of his hermitage, chatting with two middle-aged Japanese women. Dressed in a dark blue *samue*, he of course looked nothing like the Okie cowpoke I had pictured in my mind. The real Gerald Hogan was a deep-blue leprechaun, a naughty elf capable of minor mischief, perhaps, but without an ounce of harm in his entire being. At that time he was sixty-six, my father's age – a fact that almost shook me for some reason – but I thought he looked much older. Weathered and a bit feeble-looking, he was a small man with an oversized head and hands, and his intense blue eyes were set off by extremely long, bushy eyebrows that bent up and away from his face at odd angles.

The two ladies chattered on, repeatedly addressing Gerald as "*sensei*," and from their body language alone, it was obvious that they held him in high esteem. When he noticed us in the doorway, he took a long drag from a Seven Stars and called over to us in a baritone that reminded me of John Huston.

"Hello, friends. Come on in. Come right in and join us." He chose his words deliberately, and in his voice there was still a faint trace of a dusty 1930s Oklahoma drawl.

Gerald had invited us over for a day of drinking and chatting, so Mike, his new girlfriend Michiko and I stopped off at the local sake shop to get three bottles of his favorite libation. When we put the bottles on the counter, the shopkeepers, an ancient couple who looked very much like twins, immediately understood our plans for the day: "Ah … Mountain Mist … Please say hello to Hogan-*sensei* for us."

MIKE

Throughout the ten years we've known each other, it's always impressed me that a Londoner like Mike and a southern Illinois shit-kicker like myself could have so much in common. Maybe part of it is that we arrived in Japan at the same time on an international exchange program and in the first couple of years experienced the same jumps and starts and setbacks that came with adjusting to life in a foreign country. In that sense, we've more or less "grown up" together, almost like two brothers who've shared a room.

Mike was tall and lean, and although he was only thirty, his hair was already silvery-gray. He had the fresh and honest face of a ten-year-old boy, with big, beaming brown eyes and a gleaming smile worthy of a Pearl Drops ad.

Before coming to Japan, Mike had been a high school science teacher in London, and he'd traveled extensively in Europe, the Middle East and India. He knew more about politics, history and geography than any non-specialist I'd ever met. He was self-effacing, never displaying his intimate knowledge of Pakistani wedding customs, for instance, unless the subject came up naturally in conversation.

Mike had been a runner in his schooldays, and even after I met him, by which time he had taken up smoking, he would still do the occasional marathon. Once, when I went along with about a dozen other friends to watch him run, we were perplexed and then amused when he suddenly strayed from the course, dashed into a small restaurant and emerged a minute later holding a mug of beer in one hand and a lit cigar in the other. Later he told me that he'd run his fastest marathon ever that day.

There were many sides to Mike, and as he kept himself well hidden and well protected, only those closest to him were likely to see behind his comic masks. I realized soon after meeting him that beneath the absurd, manic humorist (the face he showed most often when out with people) was a serious young man of enormous sensitivity.

In 1993, I arrived in Japan with my American wife of eight years, and within the first six months we divorced. It was an amicable parting with no fireworks or nasty battles, but the adjustments were tough for me – being single for the first time in nearly a decade in a country where I couldn't read a menu or properly pronounce my own name.

Of all the people I told about the breakup, Mike took it hardest. We were sitting at a hotel bar in Kobe, a few moments after my wife and I had over the phone put the whole thing to rest. I felt neither happy nor unhappy at that moment, just relieved that it was over. I told Mike about the decision, very nonchalantly I'd thought, and I was astounded when he broke down in tears, covering his face with his hands. In the years to come, I'd understand even more fully how this unpredictable and sometimes contradictory character was a deeply sympathetic friend.

SENSEI

Forty-three years. He'd been in Japan for forty-three years. I never understood why Gerald took such pleasure in the number, but he obviously did. "Forty-three years, and it seems like yesterday," he'd say to everyone he met. On those days when I was visiting Mike at Tokudaiji, we'd call Gerald and ask if he'd mind a visit. He always urged us to come by immediately, and we would – after making the trek down the stone path into the village, where we'd procure provisions for the day: two 1.8-liter bottles of Mountain Mist, some beers, a couple of packs of cigarettes and perhaps something to eat.

When we arrived, Gerald and his *deshi* Tama-chan would greet us at the door. We'd take the provisions into the kitchen, the floor of which was always cluttered with empty bottles of

Mountain Mist. The first time I visited, taken aback by the number of "fallen soldiers," I asked Gerald if by any chance he enjoyed his drink. Without a trace of reservation, Gerald replied, "Yes, I do, actually. I permit myself one bottle a day of Mountain Mist." Sitting cross-legged in the corner behind him, an "eyebrows up" Tama-chan gave me the peace sign. Only later did I realize he'd meant to indicate "two bottles a day."

Mike, Michiko and I would sit with Gerald and let the day slip away in what the *sensei* called, with relish perhaps born of nostalgia, "shooting the breeze." The four of us talked about whatever came to mind and enjoyed the simple pleasure of being together. For the better part of one day, we reminisced about the games we'd played as children, and Gerald told us how he and his school chums used to take a piece of a two-by-four and guide a tireless bicycle wheel along the "hard road" that ran in front of the family farm. We recalled the days of hide-and-seek, kick-the-can, catching tadpoles and crawdads in their mud holes. We talked about the pleasures of stealing neighbors' watermelons, fishing for bluegill in deep-green farm ponds and riding ponies through thick woods under the light of the moon. I felt myself carried back to southern Illinois, with all of nature – the sound of crickets and tree frogs and whip-poor-wills – just beyond the screen of my bedroom window.

We rarely touched on matters of religion, but if the subject of Zen did come up, Mike and Gerald would run through a routine they'd apparently worked out.

"What will you do, Mike, when you meet the Buddha on the road?"

"Kill him, *sensei*."

"And why, Mike?"

"Because the Buddha you meet on the road won't be the Buddha."

"Oof! Exactly, Mike. That's the ticket."

One night after untold cups of Mountain Mist and several hours of shooting the breeze, Mike asked about a large hanging scroll that adorned a corner of the main hall of Gerald's hermitage. It was a frightful sight: an almost ghoulish-looking Buddha walking past a twisted oak tree, to the side of which stood a crudely drawn crimson demon figure.

"That picture says so much," Gerald said. "Not just about Zen or God, but about all of us – human beings. We've all got that great spirit, the Buddha, inside us, and right next to him is a dirty little red devil, just standing by, ready to fuck everything up. Oof!"

We all laughed hard, Gerald included, but in an instant his expression was all seriousness. "Look at that picture," he said. "You see the Buddha and the devil together. In Christianity, there's always the idea of opposites: God and Satan, heaven and hell, good and bad, right and wrong, sins and virtues. And all the ideas about following certain rules come from too much emphasis on words, on books, on written authority."

"What's right and wrong in Zen?" I asked.

"It's pretty simple," he said, looking into my eyes. "Do something that helps others – that's a virtue, a good deed. Do something that harms other people, and that's wrong. We all do both, and nobody's completely good or bad." He swallowed another cup of Mountain Mist and let out another robust "Oof!" from his dark-blue belly.

SANDY

Mike came to be staying in Tokudaiji that summer after I connected him with Sandy, a hippie-ish American woman of about thirty who was teaching some corporate English classes I had arranged. At some point she mentioned that she and her husband lived in a temple in rural Kyoto and were looking for someone to "temple-sit" during their summer in Europe. The temple was very spiritual and peaceful, she said – the perfect place for meditating and getting in touch with nature. I knew Mike wasn't the type to sit in the lotus position and recite sutras, but I thought he might like to escape from the concrete and congestion of the city during the oppressive Kansai summer. Mike was then back in London for a visit, and with a few quick phone calls, all of the arrangements were made.

My impression of Sandy – who had struck me as a bit flaky but otherwise pleasant and well spoken – suffered a severe blow one night about a week before Mike was set to return to Japan and move into the temple. Shortly before midnight, I was awakened by a phone call, and when I answered, Sandy was already in mid-sentence, almost ranting.

"Just what kind of maniac is this friend of yours, this Mike? I just phoned him to go over some last-minute details, and he's dead drunk. You know, it's still in the afternoon over there, and the guy is fucking plastered!"

"Well, I'm not there, so I don't know. Maybe he's having a farewell party with his friends before he comes back to Japan. It's not like you called him at work, you know."

"Oh, God, oh, God. What have I gotten myself into, Wil? I should never have trusted you. I don't even know you. And now I find out your friend's a fucking drunk."

"Listen, Sandy, I don't think it's necessary to start calling anybody a 'fucking drunk' based on one phone call. All I can tell you is that I've known him for five years, and he's absolutely reliable and responsible."

"And he's a goddamn booze-hound." She was now yelling into the phone, and I thought she might be coming unhinged. "I can't let this fucking drunk stay in the temple. It's a lot of responsibility. He's got to clean the place, take care of the cats . . . there's a whole daily routine. It's not a college dorm room; it's a fucking temple! Shit!"

"Listen, Sandy. I'll tell you one thing, and then I'm going back to bed. There's no law against having a few drinks in the afternoon, so far as I know. If you don't want Mike to take care of the place, then call him and tell him so. If you want him to do it, I give you my word that everything will be fine."

"Oh, shit, shit, shit. I should have known better than to trust a stranger with this. Damn it! I'm leaving in a few days, and I don't have time to get anybody else this late. You'd just better tell this guy not to be having big booze parties while we're away."

"You tell him, Sandy. I'm going to bed. Goodnight."

I did in fact, call Mike the next day, and as I had imagined, he'd met some old friends in a pub and eventually got "a bit smashed," as he put it. Mike and I agreed that Sandy's behavior was "outrageous and hysterical," and we concluded that she must have been too busy preparing for her trip to be soaking up the spiritual, peaceful atmosphere of the temple. I never doubted for a second that Mike would take good care of Tokudaiji.

The Artists

One day after Mike had moved into Tokudaiji, we were sitting on the edge of the wooden veranda, idly smoking cigars and drinking gin and tonics, when three darkly clad young people emerged at the top of the stone path. Friends of Sandy, they were members of an avant-garde *butoh* dance troupe from San Francisco who were stopping off for a couple of days on their way to a performance in Tokyo.

From the moment Kenji, the leader, pulled out his portfolio of photos, I knew Mike wouldn't be able to resist "taking the piss," as the English call it. Although he appreciated the arts (being himself a lover of theatre and opera), he had a strong distaste for artsy-fartsy types who liked to over-intellectualize everything, as he saw it. As he and I perused a shot of grimacing dancers in black tights and white face paint, their bodies contorted into grotesque attitudes, I knew what was coming.

"What was this show called?" Mike asked.

"This production was in New York. 'Kisses of Death, Screams of Joy,'" Kenji said matter-of-factly. "The actors on the right represent a praying mantis devouring a butterfly."

"Dear God in heaven, that must be excruciating," Mike said in mock astonishment. "It must take years and years to develop your instrument." I noticed with relief that they hadn't detected the irony in his voice. This was one of Mike's gifts: He could come across as fully sincere even when he was having a laugh at their expense.

"Well, it's the years of training that prepare us for the physical demands," Kenji said. "By the time we get to the actual live production, we're completely zoned and into the performance." I winced, knowing just how phrases like "zoned" would go down with Mike.

He could restrain himself no longer. "Pardon my saying so, but you have to admit, this is really fucking weird stuff." An almost maniacal grin appeared on his face. "I mean, bloody hell, everyone writhing around on the floor. It's like people playing Twister in a lunatic asylum." And for the first time, I heard Mike let out a resounding "Oof!"

For me, it was like having your classmate say "fuck" in front of your grandparents. I felt a wave of giddy nervous tension. Secretly, I found it all hilarious, but I was sure that the artists-in-black had been offended.

But I needn't have worried. Not a feather was ruffled, and in the end, we all spent a pleasant afternoon together. At first I figured they had decided that Mike had only been teasing them. Later, though, I came to believe that they had actually enjoyed his reaction. They were, after all, in the business of provoking and disturbing their audiences, and they may have relished the idea of shocking people like us.

ROBBIE

"Tell me something, Robbie. You didn't kiss that girl on the mouth, did you?" I asked the question because Robbie was a real farm boy, and no matter how long he's lived abroad or how many world capitals he's been through, some things about a country boy never change.

"Yeah, I did. What of it? "

"Considering what those girls do for a living, I think I'd rather kiss the other end," I said. There was a long silence between us.

We'd met in Kyoto that balmy afternoon for lunch, some book shopping at Maruzen and a few quick beers, but Robbie had first made his way over to the dank and cramped chambers of the Pink Lemon Salon, one of the many sex shops around Gion, the area that travel guides and the tourists who carry them unfailingly refer to as the "geisha district."

"And you talked to her after you finished?" I asked.

"You know, she starts asking me where I'm from and why I'm paying for it. So, I put my arm around her, we lean back against the wall, and she tells me all about herself. Tells me her name is Lilian. Says she's studying Portuguese and saving up to move to Brazil. She was Japanese, but for some reason I kept thinking she was Brazilian. Lilian the Brazilian."

"So, what did this all take – two hours or something?"

"No, less than an hour. After she finished, she said I was a real gentleman. I think I blushed, but I told her she was *kawaii*. When I left the place, I said the only word I know in Portuguese, '*Obrigado*,' and for some reason, I was caught off guard when she said, 'You're welcome' in English."

"Well, it sounds like you two had a lovely first date," I said.

"Fuck off. She was damned cute. Man, I can't understand why such a sweet little thing is working in a shitty place like that." I felt a little sick to hear him go on this way.

The only son of an older farming couple, Robbie was an unlikely amalgam. His conversations were a mix of lunatic hillbilly cousins getting their thumbs chomped off in wheat combines and explications of Chomsky's latest treatise on the Sandinistas and CIA conspiracies. He spoke English like you'd expect a Kansas boy to speak it, but his Japanese, pure Kansai-*ben*, was colorful and flawless. Robbie stood about six-two, with paper-white skin and blond hair straight down to his waist. Everywhere he went, someone would ask if he was a musician, and he always replied, "I'm a drummer" in an oddly misplaced, defiant tone. But true enough, he had been a member of a *taiko* group, like so many of the young expatriates we knew. Now Robbie was living in Boston and had just come to Kyoto for a week's visit.

That evening, Robbie and I were going out to Tokudaiji for a *yakiniku* and fireworks party, which we'd been planning to mark the end of Mike's time at the temple.

The Road to Tokudaiji

About fifteen locals, both native and foreign, were coming that night, along with a few of us from farther out. Robbie and I had agreed to stop off to buy an electric grill before we started the three-hour train ride. In our enthusiasm for the night's festivities, we bought two identical Teflon-coated Mitsubishi grills of about thirty inches in diameter, several pounds of beef, pork and chicken, and a couple of bags of vegetables to grill that night.

After about an hour on the way, we stopped off at a small station to meet Tim, an exceptionally tall American teacher I knew, and his oldest friend, Martin, who was visiting from New Hampshire, where he had been living on a "Zen ranch," as he called it. They were excited to be meeting Gerald, who was an almost legendary figure for many foreigners in Kansai.

Tim was around thirty years old, and I considered him sociable and pleasant but rather tightly wound. For me, he was too careful about what he ate and drank, how he conducted himself and what words left his mouth. I enjoyed talking with him about books, traveling, even women, but I felt he was a bit priggish. He often talked about romance and relationships with Japanese women but never uttered a word related to sex.

Tim was still reeling from a recent blow. Yumiko, his fiancée, had suddenly broken off their engagement when she discovered that Tim didn't eat any foods containing added sugar. She had explained that since she cooked mainly traditional Japanese dishes using soy sauce, sake and sugar, their marriage would inevitably end in unhappiness and divorce.

I recall vividly the phone call from Tim, which started with, "I can't believe what's happening. She says we can't get married because I don't like sugar! Is this woman insane?"

It was sad that they couldn't reconcile their dietary differences, but such is the banal reality of what is called "culture shock." Usually, it's not culture that shocks us, it's people, most often those we believe we know most intimately.

Tim's friend Martin I disliked immediately. He struck me as the sort of "expert *gaijin*" that I always did my best to avoid and to shun when avoidance proved impossible. Like so many Zen pilgrims, Martin fancied himself an authority on all things Japanese – particularly those things that were "really" Japanese, such as the tea ceremony, martial arts, calligraphy and, of course, Zen Buddhism.

In contrast, I had liked Robbie and Mike from the start because they were down-to-earth. The three of us shared a similar perspective on life in Japan; we were mainly interested in what I thought of as "kitchen table life," the everyday comings and goings of the average person. We had all been living in Japan for several years, and we never for a moment thought we were "studying" anything that could be called "culture."

Martin had been in the country a total of two months,

including a homestay in Tokyo in his high school days, but typical of his ilk, he knew everything about "them" as a race. Within ten minutes of our meeting at the station, Martin was boasting about picking up and screwing high school girls with the three or four set phrases he'd memorized in Japanese. True to form, as soon we got on a local bus headed in the direction of Tokudaiji, Martin was hard at work on his next conquest, a dim-looking high schooler with rusty dyed hair and the standard-issue Louis Vuitton bag. Sitting just behind Martin and forced to listen to his pickup routine, I felt almost nauseated – all the more so as it was clear that the object of his desire was in a perfect swoon over him.

When the four of us finally got off the bus (Martin with the girl's cellphone number in hand), Robbie said rather flatly, "Damn, man, don't you think she was just a bit too … underage?"

"Ah, come on. It's not like she's a virgin or anything, you know," Martin countered. "I mean, face it: Pussy's pussy." Robbie and I shared a look: there was no point in pursuing it. I never asked Tim, but I wondered how two such personalities – the prude and the perv – had ever become best friends.

In the Eyes of Buddha

Mike was there at the top of the stone steps to meet all of us. He announced that Hogan-*sensei* would be coming soon, and there was genuine anticipation in the air. While Robbie was showing Tim and Martin around the place, Mike and I started getting things ready inside the temple. As soon as they were out of earshot, Mike grabbed me by the arm.

"You won't believe what's gone on here the past couple of days," he started. From the look on his face, I knew that something good was coming.

"Last night around ten, I hear footsteps outside, and a

couple of minutes later, there she is. You remember the beautiful religious girl I've told you about – Yukari? Well she showed
up here last night – just popped in."

Mike had indeed talked about Yukari. She was a gor-
geous, well-educated woman much to his liking, but she be-
longed to some religious sect and was required by her family
to marry within that group. She'd had a huge crush on Mike all
along, but there was the problem of religion, and so Mike had
never pursued a relationship with her.

"So, she shows up with some wine and some sushi, and
she asks if she can stay the night. Of course I said yes, and in a
short while we started a fire for the bath, had a glass of wine,
and then she starts taking off her clothes."

"Okay, I see where this is going," I said, unable to hide
my glee.

"Yeah, that's where it went, but before that, we talked for
a while, and she says that she's always been in love with me, but
there's no point in starting anything serious, since her family
is in that religious group. But check this out. She made a point
of us doing it right in front of the Buddha. I was fairly pissed
anyway, but it was a bit weird to be making love on the tatami
right in front of the altar – what with the little Buddha sitting
there and all."

"So did scales fall from your eyes?"

"Yes, indeed. Most enlightening. For a beauty like her,
I'd convert in a minute – and I think in fact I offered. But there
seems to be some rule about being born into the religion. They
don't proselytize."

"It's a shame they don't," I said. "Sounds like she's got a
real talent for spreading the gospel."

"So, it's like this. I wake up at about eight in the morning,
the two of us buck naked, my knees chafed and bruised, and
I'm hearing all these voices. I rush through the place, find some
clothes to throw on, and I realize that the village residents'
group has come to pull weeds and spruce up the grounds of

the temple. They do it once a month. I'm positive that some of them saw Yukari naked in front of the altar – I could see it on their faces. Luckily, I was still a bit pissed and couldn't be bothered to be embarrassed about it."

"Well, well. Quite a busy time you've had, eh? And now you've got twenty people coming over for dinner. Take it easy tonight and try not to have any more religious awakenings for a while."

THE LAST SUPPER

Within half an hour, most of the guests, including Gerald Hogan, had arrived. Among them were a few Japanese wives of foreigners who were not in attendance, some members of an archery group that had built an impressive wooden archery stage on the temple grounds, someone's adult students of English, a couple of goofy auto-mechanics who had small bags of grass stashed inside their workshirts and various others whom I hadn't met before. Everyone brought enough food and drink to share, and the doorways of the temple were lined with bottles of beer, sake and red wine. Several of the guests also brought fireworks, which we would set off after our feast – the Last Supper, as Mike and I were calling this final get-together at Tokudaiji.

Mike was in his element now, mixing with people as they drifted in and out of the main room, where we'd made a space for everyone to gather. Michiko hadn't arrived yet (her one character flaw being habitual tardiness), and in her place I was happy to assist Mike with making sure everyone had a place to sit and something to drink.

By the time I knew it, Robbie and Gerald were in the thick of what appeared to be a most pleasant conversation. When I went over by them, I found that they were talking about how family farms were disappearing in such places as

Kansas, Oklahoma and rural Japan. They were taking turns pouring cups of Mountain Mist for each other, and before long, Gerald was punctuating the odd sentence with an "Oof!"

Once all the guests had arrived or had been accounted for, Mike and I sat down with everyone for an opening *kampai*, and the party was officially under way. As is common at such gatherings, the initial reserve among the guests quickly melted away with the eating and drinking, and on this night there was an especially festive mood in the air.

Robbie now began chatting in Japanese with an attractive young woman (who for the first five or ten minutes addressed him as "*sensei*" even though he was in fact an office worker in Boston), and I took over at Gerald's side, pouring Mountain Mist and having my own share as well. I introduced him to Tim and Martin, who immediately began discussing Buddhism and Martin's experiences on the "Zen ranch."

"I'm sorry, I don't understand. Zen ranch?" Gerald asked. Hearing Gerald say the words, I felt a surge of satisfaction, thinking that my Zen Cowboy characterization had actually been prescient in some way.

Martin explained that people from all over the world visited the Zen ranch, which sounded like a small commune, to study various matters connected with Zen, including arts and meditation. Gerald said nothing but nodded slowly and took a sip of sake.

I went off to fetch another bottle, and on the way I caught a glimpse of Robbie kissing the young woman he'd been talking to. They were standing just outside the main hall in a shadow cast by a large stone lantern. At almost the same moment, Michiko appeared at the top of the stone steps, and I began teasing her, as always, about her late arrival.

When Michiko and I stepped into the main hall, the first distinguishable word I heard was satori. Martin was talking to Gerald about the path to enlightenment, and for the next few minutes, Martin pounded the satori drum like Kerouac banging on about enlightenment in *Dharma Bums*: satori, satori, satori.

After listening silently for quite a spell, Gerald cocked his head slightly to one side and spoke. "Boys, it just doesn't work that way." He said it purely without emotion. "A lot of the Western fascination with Zen is really about words and riddles, but Zen is a way of life." I thought of Gerald's way of life: forty-three years. More than fifteen-thousand mornings, days and nights in this land so far from Stillwater, Oklahoma.

Martin didn't look satisfied. He wasn't getting the answers he wanted. "But it's only through words that we can make sense of concepts and discuss them, isn't it," Martin said. "I've studied Zen, too, and I know there are different theories and approaches. Your ideas are just one way of looking at it."

I thought he was insolent and altogether full of himself, and I felt a nasty urge to put him in his place. "So, Martin-*sensei*, what makes you the authority on everything? How many weeks have you been in Japan now?"

Before Martin could respond, though, Mike broke in with an exaggerated gesture, his left arm sweeping out in a dramatic flourish. "No, no. Let him speak. For Martin is a young man, and young men must have their say." Realizing that Mike was doing a bit from *Lawrence of Arabia*, I burst out laughing, but the sour looks on the faces of Martin and Tim made it clear that that brand of humor wasn't appreciated.

"May I ask you something, *sensei*?" Tim said. His manner showed that he was genuinely interested in what Gerald would have to say.

Gerald nodded. "I'm all ears." I then noticed for the first time that his ears were huge, far out of proportion even with his very large head.

"In your opinion, of all the people here, which of us could achieve enlightenment?"

Gerald was noticeably uncomfortable. "Maybe all of us. Maybe none of us. It's not for me or anyone else to decide things like that."

"But if you had to say, who would it be? Any of us?"

There was a long pause before Gerald answered. "Well, if there's someone that I'd say was most likely, I'd have to say that it would be Wil here." He turned and looked directly at me, and although I expected him to smile or to break into laughter, he didn't.

"Oh, fuck me," Martin said under his breath.

Tim, too, was clearly shocked, and I thought he looked almost sad. I felt the blood rush to my head, and I knew my face was very red.

"Me? Why me? I've never even thought about satori once in my life," I protested.

"It's not about studying anything or trying to reach a goal," Gerald said, speaking to the whole group of us. "It's just that from talking to him, I feel that Wil is open to people and ideas."

"Oh, Jesus Christ, I don't fucking believe this," Martin said, looking down and shaking his head from side to side.

My own feelings were mixed. It was true that I'd never given a moment's thought to Zen enlightenment, but getting the *sensei*'s stamp of approval was very flattering to my ego.

More gratifying, though, was that Martin the Zen Pilgrim, the Zen Pretender, had been forced to witness it.

This was what I wanted those phony bastards to realize: Some of us *live* here, and that means something, even though it doesn't sound exotic or esoteric. All your talk about "Japan" and the "Japanese," about "Zen this" and "satori that" – you don't know a thing about it, you pretentious pricks.

Gerald then spoke in a perfectly natural tone, apparently oblivious to the tension that was making everyone else ill at ease. "Well, I think we can all agree that we do experience some things directly. And at times we don't need words to communicate," he said. He paused for a moment as if to gather his thoughts and then added, "I think sex is a good example of that." It seemed he was going to continue with this idea, but instead he let out a booming "Oof!"

HANABI

The party went on, and at some point the guests drifted into small circles of three or four. In one corner of the room, Mike, Michiko, Gerald and I were talking about Sandy's imminent return to Tokudaiji and bemoaning Mike's departure from the place, which I'd somehow never thought of as Sandy's. For me, it had become Mike's place, and in my mind, it would stay that way.

"Sandy's going to be back in a few days," Michiko said. "And that'll be the end of Mike's time here." Gerald seemed somewhat surprised by that, and I thought perhaps he'd forgotten who actually lived at Tokudaiji.

"Sometimes I don't like that woman," he said suddenly. "She calls me 'honey pie' and talks down to me because I'm a homosexual. Honey pie. Oof!" I noticed then that Gerald appeared quite drunk. He reached over to get a cigarette and something fell out of his pants pocket. It looked like a small polished stone.

"You've dropped something there, Gerald," I said.

"It's my jade snuff box. All the Chinese gentlemen carry one in their pocket," he explained. It sounded perfectly reasonable at the time, the way he said it, but later I had to wonder: what possible connection could there be between "all the Chinese gentlemen" and this Oklahoma Zen Cowboy Priest?

On the other side of the room, nearer the main doorway, Tim and Martin were talking with the mechanics and a couple of young women, and I could tell that the conversation was about the little bags of stash. It seemed the mechanics couldn't decide whether it was safe to break it out and light up.

As things turned out, they never had a chance to decide. Someone had apparently suggested that it was time for the fireworks, and I rather absently noticed that a few people were holding brightly colored packages of sparklers, bottle rockets and firecrackers. What I didn't notice was what Martin was up to.

What I recall most clearly is the wild look in Mike's eyes. It was disbelief, astonishment, panic. As he dashed toward the doorway, he shouted, "Wil, look at what this crazy son of a bitch is doing!" When I turned, I saw Martin, still seated and facing us, holding a lit Roman candle in his right hand. I shuddered in shock and then froze. He was pointing the thing directly at our faces.

Mike's words were still ringing in my ears when he knocked Martin back with what looked like some rugby blocking maneuver. There was a dull thumping sound and then the first bright ball of sparks, sulfuric yellow, shot straight up, hitting the underside of the overhang of the roof. The next burst was reddish purple, and by that time, Mike had kicked the Roman candle out across the white gravel, outside the temple hall.

By the time I realized what was happening, Mike had Martin pinned up against the temple wall, his forearm across Martin's throat. "You fucking maniac! You could've burnt the whole place to the ground!" Periodic bursts of variously colored sparks were sidling across the gravel, into the surrounding pine groves.

I heard a crunching sound, and when I looked over, Tim was rushing toward them on bare feet, as if to come to Martin's aid. "No violence! No violence!" he was yelling.

"No violence?" I screamed. "After your friend sets off fireworks inside a three-hundred-year-old wooden temple? You must be joking, you stupid asshole!"

"Get the fuck out of here and don't come back, you ignorant fucking wankers!" Mike shouted. There was a mad mix of fury and uncontestable authority in Mike's voice, and Tim and Martin obediently headed toward the stone path. Within moments, the sounds of their footsteps had faded.

I looked around, and there were only three of us left: Mike, Michiko and I. "Where's Robbie?" I asked. I realized that I hadn't seen him for some time. For the next ten minutes, we went through the temple and around it, searching for Robbie. I wondered if he might have gone off to the attractive girl's place for the night.

When we'd been twice around the temple grounds, in the darkness as black as pitch under the heavy canopy of trees, we were ready to give up. Then, seemingly out of nowhere, there came a call: "Reconciliation."

The sound came again, each syllable pronounced slowly, in a breathy whisper: "Reconciliation. Reconciliation."

Moving toward the source of the sound, Mike and I found ourselves standing directly in front of a small red *torii*, from which was hanging the pallid figure of a shirtless Robbie, his long arms looped over one of the crossbars. The sight of him was chilling. He was the perfect image of the crucifixion.

"Get off that thing, you sick bastard. We've been hunting all over for you," I said. Robbie at last lifted his head and gave us a wild-eyed grin.

"I thirst," he said.

"Then come down from there and let's have a fucking drink," Mike yelled. We all laughed, and Robbie hopped down jauntily from the *torii*. We were all laughing, but something had changed when that Roman candle went off inside Tokudai-ji. Something fine and simple had been spoiled.

Mike, Michiko, Robbie and I spent most of that night sitting on the veranda talking about Martin and how he'd ruined the Last Supper. We drank cups of Mountain Mist and gazed out into the black void of the night until the gray light of dawn gradually arrived at Tokudaiji. From time to time, one of us would light a sparkler and twirl it slowly in loops and arcs.

We all slept on the tatami of the main hall, and when we awoke the next afternoon, we decided to take the ten-minute walk through thick woods to Gerald's place to say farewell. Once we got there, we spent the next few hours drinking and shooting the breeze, but everyone took care to avoid mentioning the night before.

"Hey, what ever happened to Kenji and the dancers?" I asked.

Mike gave me a silly grin. The archery group had come one day for practice, he said, to find the three dancers rehearsing on the archery stage.

"The archers told me about it. They see these characters flailing around and bounding all over the archery stage, and they assume they're my drunken friends acting insane. They get really upset about it and start yelling at them to get the hell out of there. By the time someone told them they were actually *butoh* dancers, Kenji and his friends had already left for Tokyo."

While we sat chatting over the next hour or so, Gerald looked increasingly tired and sleepy, and when he dozed off, Michiko covered him with one of his cotton jackets, and we headed for the door. Just as Robbie started sliding the door to open it, Gerald got up and urged us to stay longer.

"No, really, we should get back to Tokudaiji," Mike said. "It's been a long couple of days, and I'm knackered." Gerald looked disappointed, but as he was intoxicated, almost staggering, I figured he wouldn't remember our departure anyway. We repeated our goodbyes and headed for the door.

As I began to step outside, Gerald moved along side me and put his arm around my neck. Before I could react, the smell of Aqua-Velva – or was it Old Spice? – was in my face, and Gerald was kissing me on the neck just below my right ear. At the same moment, I realized that he was clutching my cock through my thin cotton slacks. The strange image flashed through my mind of a blind man holding on to his white cane, and I let out a nervous giggle.

"I think he likes you, Wil," Michiko said devilishly, as if Gerald were some shaggy, affectionate dog that was rubbing up against my leg.

"Uhm, Gerald … Gerald. I'm sorry, but … " I freed myself from his grasp, top and bottom. I didn't know whether to apologize for rejecting his advances or to laugh out loud at all of it, everything that was connected to Tokudaiji.

Before I could decide anything, Gerald put his face up close to mine again and whispered confidentially, "There are many kinds of love, Wil," as though he were sharing with me the secret of the universe.

G L O S S A R Y
illustrations by peyote

anime 213
アニメ

> An abbreviated form of "animation." In Japan, the term applies to all forms of animation – crude or sophisticated – from *Doraemon* to Hayao Miyazaki's *Spirited Away*. In English, *anime* has come to be known as a Japanese invention, with its colorful and highly stylized form of animation and story lines that are often violent. Before the term *anime* entered the Japanese vocabulary, illustrated characters – animated or otherwise – were referred to as *manga*.

arigato gozaimasu 70
有り難うございます

> Thank you, polite form. Add *dohmo* to the front, and you have "thank you very much." In a more casual setting, you can say, "*Dohmo arigato*" (like in that Styx song), and among friends you can just say, "*Dohmo*." If you say, "*Dohmo, dohmo*," you will sound like a salaryman. And if you say, "Doomi arigati," you will sound like the mayor of Hayward, California, in 1986, as he addressed the student body at Ichiritsu Funabashi High School.

arubaito 35
アルバイト

> Part-time work. Comes from the German word for work, *arbeit*. We wonder if this makes Germans mad.

bakayaro 69
バカヤロ

> Idiot! Along with just plain *baka*, it is probably the most common putdown in Japanese. Different Japanese-English dictionaries offer the following translations: asshead, asshole, dumb-ass, fool, goose, moron, old socks, simpleton and, from the fourth edition of *Kenkyusha's New Japanese-English Dictionary*, you goddam simp!

-ben 184
弁

A dialect or accent. The most famous dialect in Japan is Osaka-*ben*, the language of the second city. It tends to be a little rougher around the edges than standard speech. A typical greeting in Osaka-*ben* would be "*Moukarimakka?*" which means, "Makin' any money?" The typical reply is, "*Bochibochidenna,*" which can be rendered as, "A little." If you're a foreigner with a good singing voice who's about to sing karaoke somewhere in the north of Japan, use a trick from journalist Dan Sloan's playbook and greet the audience with "*Oban de gozaimasu,*" which is "Good evening" in Tohoku-*ben*. It's sure to get a warm reception.

bento **39**
弁当

bon-odori 223
盆踊り

A Bon festival dance. This festival is held every July or August for about a week to welcome back the souls of the dead. People dress in kimono and *yukata*. The dance is held outside at night. Despite being associated with the coming back of the dead, it is an upbeat, happy dance, and usually there is a carnival-like atmosphere with booths selling food and trinkets.

butoh　181, 195
舞踏

A form of modern dance begun in 1959. Dancers usually wear white makeup. The first *butoh* performance involved a dancer simulating sex with a live chicken and breaking its neck. Since then, *butoh* proponents seem to instinctively veer toward obtuse descriptions of their art – "the polymorphic body in a mysterious ceremony," "*Butoh* is to become the other, not to mean the other," or "It's about the human experience" – as if the whole community is in denial about that chicken.

Christmas in Japan 132

The yuletide spirit often manifests itself in odd ways in Japan. At Christmas time, the KFC outlets cloak Colonel Sanders in a Santa suit. A well known department store once featured an enormous banner for the holidays that read, "SUCCESS CHRISTMAS!" And in another department store in the late eighties, our Chin Music correspondent was surprised to find among the ornaments a jolly, smiling Santa … hanging on a cross. This odd blend of the mythical and religious struck him as intriguing. Regrettably, he has yet to find an ornament in the shape of a reindeer-powered sleigh driven by Jesus in a loincloth.

deshi 177
弟子

> An adherent, apprentice, disciple or student. The master and *deshi* play a crucial role in Zen Buddhism. In a very secretive ceremony known as "the transmission" in the temple's main hall, the Zen master will transfer his esoteric teachings to a *deshi* deemed ready to receive such wisdom.

dohmo 158, 198
どうも

> Thanks, informal. This is an all-purpose term that can get you further than even *prego* does in Italy.

DV 153, 154

> Domestic violence. Little attention was given to this widespread social problem until recently. A study by the Justice Ministry found that the average age of perpetrators of domestic violence is forty. They have also been abusing family members for an average of six years. And more than forty percent of the cases of domestic violence occur in front of children. Until 2001, there was little government support for victims of domestic violence. A different study by the ministry found that one in five victims of domestic violence tried to reach out to police or family members for protection, but received no help and were beaten anyway.

fashion health 103
ファッションヘルス

> Neither fashionable, nor particularly healthy, this is the Japanese euphemism for a whorehouse.

freeter (fureeta) 35
フリーター

> They are the happily unrepresented faction of Japanese

usually in their mid-twenties working part time jobs and enjoying life. To the untrained eye one might erroneously define them as hippies. However there's something entirely more edgy and interesting about these *fureeta* than can be found under the skin of most modern Phish lovers. They abhor the salaryman work-till-you-drop corporate devotion that their parents and most of their peers embrace. They lack the overwhelming designer label obsession that has made Japan famous but can still appreciate a good pair of Gucci jeans.

They may live in Ebisu, but unlike the investment banker next door, their rent isn't six-thousand dollars a month. It's more like two-hundred dollars a month with a bath one hundred meters up the street and available at three bucks a pop.

They may work for a three-month stretch as a foreign jazz ensemble tour coordinator, one day living in lavish hotels and sipping gin and tonics next to Tito Puentes, only to pack up the next day and live on a small uninhabited island off the southern coast of Okinawa. When they arrive on this island, they may find that it is actually inhabited – by a small naked man who lives in a series of circus tents given to him by local fishermen and drug traffickers.

They may have visited over eighty countries by the age of twenty-six simply by working to travel. They may have spent two nights at the North Pole and lost a pinky toe. They may have reverse-mugged a mugger in NYC who called them a Jap but was unaware that this Jap actually *was* a black belt in karate.

While the swankster hip of Tokyo are off sniffing cocaine and popping pills in the bathrooms of Roppongi nightclubs, the *fureeta* are sitting on tatami mats in well-lived-in eighteen-square-meter rooms, smoking weed imported from Thailand and listening to reggae. They are the simple-living, good-music-sex-and-travel-craving chunk of Tokyo that nobody ever hears from because they don't care if they're heard or not. They aren't preaching one thing and living another. They aren't preaching. They're just living.

gaijin **36, 69, 128, 185**
外人

A controversial term that literally means "outside person." The word is used to describe foreigners, but especially those from Western nations. The foreign community in Japan alternately abhors and embraces the term (Foreigners often call themselves *henna gaijin*, for example, which loosely translates to "weird foreigner"). Japanese with foreign friends often try to play it safe by saying "*gaijin-san*" (Mr. or Ms. Foreigner) or "*gaikokujin*" (person from a foreign country). A member of the Chin Music Press team was greeted by chants of "*baka gaijin*" (foolish foreigner) every morning in the mid-1980s by a particularly obnoxious four-year-old boy. The boy would stand in a big patch of dirt next to the *baka gaijin*'s apartment and yell "*baka gaijin, baka gaijin, baka gaijin*" as the twenty-two-year-old man made his way to the Funabashi City Hall where he worked. The man is not particularly proud of how he handled this situation, especially now that he has three children of his own and can see how fragile a four-year-old psyche can be. After days of being called a fool on his way to work, the twenty-two-year-old ripped a toy train out of the four-year-old's hand and locked it inside his apartment. The boy ran home to his parents in tears. For several days, the twenty-two-year-old taunted the four-year-old by calling him "*omiyage-chan,*" which doesn't really translate but for our purposes we'll use "little souvenir kid." The boy slowly became fascinated with the twenty-two-year-old, staring at him from a distance whenever the man would leave his apartment. And after a few days, the man left the toy train on the stoop for the boy to retrieve. There was no more taunting by either side.

genkan 72
玄関

An entryway or vestibule. At house parties, shoes often form a jambalaya in this space, creating an excellent setting in which people can make meaningful eye contact while rummaging for their footwear. "Oop!" you say, if not drunkenly then very close, when your hand brushes against hers as you grope for your missing sandal. "*Gomen!*" she blurts in apology.

gomen 204
ごめん

An informal, even gentle, way of saying, "I'm sorry," "excuse me," or "pardon me." Of course, the girl in the *genkan* wasn't sorry. She had been checking him out ever since he arrived three hours earlier, mutely clutching two plastic bags pendulous with the weight of a dozen Ebisu tall boys. There was something … interesting about the way his eyes lolled unmoored in their sockets, like a pair of seasick marbles unable to find a purchase on anything. Unbeknownst to her, his eyes often alighted on her profile and, once or twice, her ass. He always saved his glances for those glorious moments when she threw her head back and unfurled the most amazing chortle, deep and flatulent, a sound that could split and replicate. It was a sexy laugh, so unguarded, and he wanted to hear more of it. Five cans of Ebisu helped anchor his eyes, which were now staring into hers. It turns out both of them lived along the Keio line, and it was getting late, so they decided to leave together. When their hands touched in the entryway, neurons in their temporal lobes connected to create pathways for new emotions and reinforce old ones, and as their mouths parted in ultra-slow motion to release bovine bleats drawn out like taffy, a single word crackled in their brains at the speed of light: *skinship*.

hanabi **192**
花火

Fireworks, written with the characters for "flower" and "fire." Summer fireworks displays are huge events in Japan. People dress in *yukata* and gather by the thousands – sometimes the hundreds of thousands – along riverbanks to see rival fireworks firms compete. The Sumida River display in Tokyo, which dates back to the early eighteenth century, blows up twenty-thousand fireworks each year. It's breathtaking. Sometimes you can hear Japanese yelling "Tamaya! Kagiya!" as the fireworks explode. The Kagiya clan was responsible for the very first Sumida display in 1733. The Tamayas emerged as rivals in 1810, and both clans tried to outdo each other every summer at the festival. Unfortunately, the Tamaya clan started a fire in the mid-nineteenth century that burned down its factory and neighboring homes. They were promptly kicked out of Tokyo for that, ending the famous rivalry. But other firms around the country keep the tradition alive today, giving many of the fireworks shows in Japan an edge they lack elsewhere. Also, during the summer, families light off sparklers and little bottle rockets in their driveways – just about every convenience store sells them.

hikikomori 41
引きこもり

Refers to someone who stays in his or her home or room to an excessive degree. Similar in meaning to recluse. The word became popular in the late 1990s as some young people, mostly male, secluded themselves in their rooms and became modern-day hermits. While some journalists and doctors say as many as one million young people qualify as *hikikomori*, others argue that these estimates are inflated by people who have a vested interest in seeing the phenomenon flourish. Definitions of the term tend to be vague. For example, young people who aren't going to school and don't have a job sometimes refer to themselves as *hikikomori* even though they are not shutting themselves in their rooms. For those who are serious shut-ins, parents often leave food by the door and are reluctant to intervene with the child, doctors say. The worst of the cases lead to domestic violence, but more often, young people live quietly in their rooms, only coming out after dark, if at all.

honban 103
本番

In acting, this is a take or a live performance, not a rehearsal. In the sex industry, it's a euphemism for having sex.

honne 37, 38
本音

One's true intentions. Often used in contrast to *tatemae*.

i-mode 162

This platform for surfing the Net via one's cellphone was introduced in February 1999 by NTT DoCoMo. It quickly caught on with Japanese youth and became the biggest fad since karaoke or PlayStation 2. Soon after the launch of i-mode, Japanese teenagers were being called "the thumb generation" because they spent so much time tapping out commands on their tiny cellphone keypads. By early 2004, i-mode had more than forty million users, or about one in every four Japanese.

irasshaimase 33
いらっしゃいませ

Welcome. You'll often hear this greeting, or the shortened *irasshai*, as you enter a store, restaurant or bar in Japan. Sometimes the whole staff seems to be yelling it, which can take a newcomer aback. One of the worst inventions of all time is a machine that repeats a high-pitched "*irasshaimase*" as a person enters a store and an "*arigato gozaimashita*" (thank you very much) as he or she leaves. There is a liquor store in the Yoga neighborhood of Tokyo that has one of these – the elderly couple who run the shop are evidently too busy to say the greetings themselves. But of course, the machine gets mixed up and says "*irasshaimase*" as you leave at least half the time. The shop is small, and the cash register is near the door, so when you pay for your beer or sake, you can stand close to the door and set the machine off in a wild frenzy of "*irrashaimase*" and "*arigato gozaimashita*." No matter how long you do this, the shopkeepers will show no sign whatsoever that anything is wrong.

izakaya 30
居酒屋

A Japanese pub that usually has an extensive menu of little dishes to choose from. They range from vast places teeming with drunken college kids to quiet hideaways perfect for a double date. The typical drinks here are beer and *shochu*, a distilled alcoholic beverage. Several of the non-Japanese contributors to this book learned most of their Japanese in *izakaya*. If you visit an *izakaya*, we would be very proud if you try this: when the waiter or waitress comes around for your order, say, "Mick Jagger." Put your best Japanese accent on it: "mikku jagga." If you are served a dish of beef and potatoes, you win.

jisatsu-keijiban 109
自殺掲示板

Internet bulletin boards focused on suicide. The sites explain how to commit suicide and allow people to swap messages. Strangers meet through the sites and schedule joint suicides so that they won't die alone.

kampai 189
乾杯

Cheers!

karoshi 39
過労死

Death from overwork. While some people just collapse and die from overwork (the government recognized 143 cases of *karoshi* in fiscal 2001), others are driven to suicide because of their work, a death known as *karojisatsu* (*karoshi* + *jisatsu* or suicide). A key legal case in 2000 found advertising giant Dentsu responsible for the *karojisatsu* of one of its young male employees. The man, a recent college grad, quickly found that he could not keep up with his workload, and after just a few months on the job, began staying all night to finish his work. Near the end of his first year at Dentsu, his supervisor told him to go home and get some sleep, but in the summer of 1991, he was still working until six thirty in the morning on occasions and was averaging two hours of sleep a night. He began driving erratically and acting abnormally, and near the end of August of that year, he hanged himself at his family home. The family sued and, after a series of appeals, the Supreme Court ruled that

Dentsu had to pay compensation of 169 million yen to the family. This was the first time a company was held liable for a case of *karojisatsu*.

kawaii **183**
かわいい

Cute, charming, adorable.

keitai denwa **34**
携帯電話

kireru **44**
切れる

To lose it, snap, reach a breaking point. Often accompanied with an act of violence.

konnichiwa **69**
こんにちは

Good afternoon, hello. A common greeting. Even the mayor of Hayward, California, can say it.

nama fera **103**
生フェラ

Twin brothers Toby and Glen wore their purple and gold lettermen jackets to Tokyo. It was a long ways from Missoula, and in the no̱-moon darkness they felt like kings of another planet. Twelve steps down a garish, claustrophobic street, Toby, the more squat of the two, was pulled by his gold leather sleeve into a humid foyer. Glen, older by four minutes, did a little sideways hop-step and followed his brother in. Twenty-four minutes later, they emerged with the biggest pair of rictus grins you've ever seen. Fifty-two years later, all it would take was for Toby to shoot his brother a crafty look and say, "Dude, *nama fera*," and they would snort and jab each other with their bony elbows. Sometimes, a grandkid would ask them what that meant, and Glen – it was always Glen – would say, "Look it up, little man."

natto **75**
納豆

A food product made of fermented soybeans. *Natto* is not glutinous. Rather, it is sticky and soft, so perhaps "gloppy" is a better characterization. Non-Japanese are supposed to hate *natto*. It is kind of a rule. To enjoy *natto* is an act of defiance. The Japanese will often make funny noises if you tell them you eat it regularly, usually letting forth a downward arcing "heeeeeeey!" sound. Maybe it is better to describe the "heeeeeeey!" sound as slowly undulating. It's an undulatory, extended "hey!" Vegetarians can (somewhat defensively) claim to eat it for the excellent source of protein that it is. Eaten plain, *natto* is just shy of revolting. Most connoisseurs prefer to mix it vigorously with a savory sauce called *dashi*, a dab of hot mustard and some seaweed, then pour it atop a bowl of hot rice. Snot-like, *natto* smells like a fourteen-year-old boy's sock.

nihongo jozu desu ne. 70
日本語上手ですね。

"Your Japanese is good." Although there is no scientific evidence to support this claim, it is generally accepted that there is an exact negative correlation between the frequency with which this sentence is said in response to one's attempts to speak Japanese and one's actual language skills. In other words, when you stop hearing this sentence, your Japanese is good.

obasan 33
叔母さん

Aunt or middle-aged woman. *Obaasan* means grand-mother. Either way, they are the salt of the earth, and we love them.

ocha 108
お茶

ohayo 158
おはよう

> "Good morning." We can almost picture the mayor of Hayward, California, trying to get back on track after that debacle at the high school (see *arigato gozaimasu*), as he strides into the Funabashi mayor's office at nine AM sharp and belts out a breezy, "Iowa!"

onsen 76, 102
温泉

(o)soshiki 68
お葬式

> A funeral. The *o* is honorific. The Japanese almost all opt to be cremated after death. The figure is something like ninety-eight or ninety-nine percent. After the funeral ceremony, family and friends of the deceased will proceed to the crematorium, where the body is incinerated. Once the deceased has been reduced to ashes and bones, loved ones pick up the bones with chopsticks and place them in a jar. The hyoid bone in the larynx is considered special because it resembles Buddha in prayer. After the bones have been put in a jar, the people in attendance usually hold a party in honor of the deceased. For a good cinematic portrayal of the customs surrounding a Japanese funeral, check out Akira Kurosawa's *Ikiru* or Juzo Itami's *Ososhiki*.

otaku 101
お宅

> Nerd, freak. This word is also a polite way to say "your house," but in the early 1980s, it began morphing into its current, more prevalent meaning. Journalist Akio Nakamori wrote a series of articles in 1983 entitled "The Study of *Otaku*" (*Otaku no Kenkyuu*) that talked about the qualities of hardcore *anime, manga* and video game fans. The term took on a more sinister twist in 1989, when Tsutomu Miyazaki was arrested for the murder of four preteen girls. His apartment was littered with thousands of *anime* videos and *manga*, including slasher films, rape fantasies and other hardcore porn. In 1992, the term was lobbed across the Pacific with a much more positive spin with the North America release of the *anime* classic *Otaku no Video*. This animated film tells the story of disaffected youth who find joy in creating *anime*. Promotion of the movie included this call to arms: "Fight! OtaKing! Defend the hopes and dreams of *otaku* everywhere!"

ote 126
お手

> Shake. A command used by dog owners to get their pets to raise their paws. On New Year's 2006, the next Year of the Dog, temple grounds nationwide will be teeming with dogs and their owners as they make their first prayer of the year together.

otsuya 68
お通夜

> Literally the "holy transit evening." This is a Japanese wake. Some are held at home and others are held at funeral parlors.

oyaji-gari **30, 39**
親父狩り又は親爺狩り

Geezer-hunting, old-man-hunting, father-hunting. The practice of young teens beating up and robbing older white-collar men. Sometimes the violence is random. Other times, the men are set up by girls posing as prostitutes. The term has been in use since the mid 1990s.

puchi-iede **103**
プチ家出

Petite runaway, a hybrid of French and Japanese. Refers to young schoolgirls who leave home for days at a time with the intention of eventually returning. Sometimes they are said to sell their bodies to make money for shopping. This is the kind of thing news organizations salivate over. Yet the stories are almost always anecdotal. Somehow they can figure out how many foreigners committed crimes on any given week in Japan, but they can't tell us how many of their daughters turn tricks for Louis Vuitton bags! I mean, what is going on here?!!! (*Chin Music Press team intervenes, slapping writer across the face several times, screaming, "Get a grip, man, get a grip!! It's over now. You're in the United States of America."*) Sorry … I apologize. Just another flashback.

rajio taiso **76**
ラジオ体操

Literally, "radio exercise." An exercise program broadcast over the radio in Japan. It has been aired every day since 1928, with the exception of eight days from August fifteenth to the twenty-second, 1945, when the program took a break for obvious reasons. *Rajio taiso* was started by a government organization to keep the populace in tip-top shape. On the show, a piano plays as an energetic man leads people in light calisthenics. Some companies still start the day with a session of *rajio taiso*; others do it at three PM, just when everyone is starting to go into their post-lunch doze. Neighbors also gather to do the exercises in the early morning during the summer holidays. But many companies have stopped the tradition, and, frankly, the young generation considers *rajio taiso* a bit of a joke. It's kind of like dancing to a Lawrence Welk record or doing one of those German beer hall dances where everyone clucks and squats. Visitors to Japan often find *rajio taiso* an amusing affirmation of their stereotypes of the country. But the show's little secret is that it's actually American. The first program was aired in 1925 from the New York headquarters of Metropolitan Life Insurance. Sometime around the stock market crash and the ensuing Great Depression, American interests turned from radio exercises to finding food to eat. But in Japan, the program just kept building in popularity. By 1962, Japan was holding *rajio taiso* demonstrations of ten million strong.

sake **174, 207**
酒

sakura **97, 98**
桜

Cherry blossoms. The appearance of these flowers in early spring triggers a week of outdoor parties, where people drink, dance, eat and sing under the blossoms. A good idea for a Japan book with a picaresque edge would be to start a trip in southern Kyushu and follow the cherry blossoms north, partying all the way.

salaryman **17, 75**
サラリーマン

samue **175**
さむえ

Clothing traditionally worn by priests, monks and artisans. Made of cotton and linen, it's more durable than a *yukata*.

san man nin 108
三万人

> Thirty-thousand people. At least that many people have killed themselves every year in Japan since 1998. While talk of Japan's high suicide rate used to be based partly on myth, it is now very real.

sayonara party 164

> A farewell party. This isn't really a Japanese term – it's more of a hybrid of Japanese and expat-ese. Incidentally, the term "*sayonara* home run" to indicate a game-ending homer in baseball is far superior to the clinical "walk-off home run" used these days, don't you think?

sensei 175, 178, 186, 189, 190
先生

Seven Stars **94**

shiitake **109**
しいたけ

A type of mushroom. From the Chin Music kitchen: lightly brown half a pound of halved *shiitake* in about a tablespoon of butter. Before turning off the heat, add about a tablespoon of soy sauce. Turn off the heat. Eat.

shimei **101**
指名

A nomination, designation or request. Used in politics, business and brothels.

shiso **92, 99**
紫蘇

A beefsteak plant. Reminds us of a favorite dish:
(serves two)
1 strip of raw *tarako* (salted cod roe)
1 *shiso* leaf
1 table spoon of butter
a splash of white wine
spaghetti

Pop open the *tarako* with a fork and empty the contents into a small bowl. Mix with melted butter, adding a splash of white wine, until smooth. Toss mixture with cooked spaghetti. Chop *shiso* into thin strips and sprinkle over the spaghetti. Add salt and pepper to taste.

skinship (sukinshippu) 205
スキンシップ

A melding of the word "skin" and the suffix "ship," it refers to physical contact between two people and the attendant feelings of affection it creates. As the pair glided under a canopy of reddening zelvokas, all the evening's random thoughts were melted down into a titanium BB engraved with the words, "I want to hold your hand." He heard his voice repeat those words and felt her fingers, small and warm, lace between his, big and clammy. They laughed.

taiko 184
太鼓

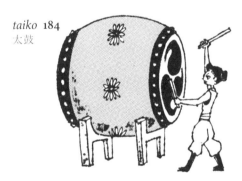

tarento 104
タレント

Basically a TV personality, although definitions vary. If you've ever seen someone on TV a lot and wondered what that person *really* does for a living, he or she is probably a *tarento*. Westerners worthy of being called *tarento* include: Pia Zadora, the Osborne family and Ted Koppel.

tatemae **37, 38**
建て前

Sometimes called a façade, an official stance, a policy. Also refers to a house's frame. Contrasts with *honne*, one's true intentions or beliefs.

tetsugakuteki jisatsu **110**
哲学的自殺

Philosophical suicide. Misao Fujimura, an eighteen-year-old student in Tokyo, left the first philosophical suicide note before killing himself at Kegon Falls in 1904. In his note, Fujimura passionately refuted the idea that modern Western science and rationalization, just then getting a firm foothold in Japan, could explain away all of life's mystery.

torii **194**
鳥居

toro **92, 100**
とろ

The fatty flesh of tuna. Often caught in nets off the coast of Chile, pulled aboard and spiked in the brain, then laid out on a grass mat or blanket so the two-hundred-kilogram fish won't bruise. The bluefin is then refrigerated and flown to Tokyo. Once it arrives, the fish is lined up with its compatriots on the cold concrete at Tsukiji, the world's largest fish market, at about three in the morning. Potential buyers begin to check the tuna around four. They use a flashlight and sharp little hooks to cut open the tuna near its tail and check the marbling and color of the flesh. Around half-past five, the auction begins. If the tuna is good quality, it will bring around ten-thousand yen a kilogram. Once the fish is bought, the buyers will paint a number or symbol on it and later cart it off to a restaurant or market.

Uniqlo **136**

A retail chain famous for low-priced fleece jackets and jeans. The clothes are produced in China. Several years ago, Uniqlo was the rising star of Japanese retail, and Tadashi Yanai, the company's founder, was heralded as a visionary. In 2002, he ranked twelfth on the *Asiaweek* list of the top fifty powerful people in the region. "The bigger the casual brand market in a country, the more advanced the society is as a democracy," Yanai said then. Lately, the brand has lost its luster.

wa **124, 125, 127**

和

Harmony, unity, concord. When the star pitcher of the Press Club Alley Cats in Tokyo defected in spring 2004 to a rival softball team, he told the manager that the Cats didn't have *wa* anymore. Manager Patrick Killen later remarked, "I don't remember anyone by that name."

yakiniku 184
焼肉

Korean barbecue. Cook the thin slices of meat, tongue and vegetables at your table. And don't forget the kimchi.

yakuza 103
やくざ

yamamba 35
山姥

yukata 200, 216
浴衣

> A light cotton robe, usually worn in summer. Blue and white *yukata* are standard issue at Japanese inns and hot springs resorts. Make sure the right side of the robe goes on the outside (or was it the left side?), so you won't be mistaken for a corpse. Also, if you are new to Japan and a neighbor presents you with a *yukata* and tells you that everyone will be wearing one at the *bon-odori* festivities that night, be warned: You are definitely being set up. In fact, you may be the only one wearing a *yukata*, with the exception of a few elderly ladies, and you may look and feel like an idiot. Also, because you don't really know how to wear one of these robes, you may inadvertently show way more flesh than a Japanese would – if they actually wore these robes. However, one good thing will come of all this: That night will be seared onto your memory as if it happened yesterday, not in 1986.

yuzu 104, 105
柚

> The fruit of the citron tree, sometimes called a Chinese lemon.

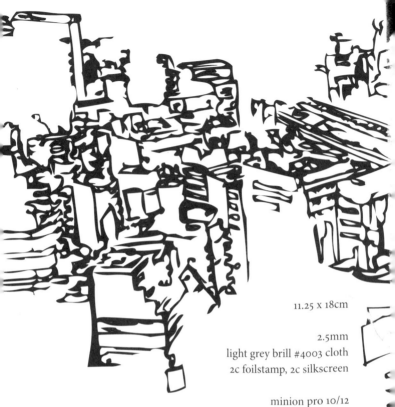

11.25 x 18cm

2.5mm
light grey brill #4003 cloth
2c foilstamp, 2c silkscreen

minion pro 10/12
120g munken pure

hold cover up to window :
tokyo l-tower 28th floor
nishi-shinjuku
shinjuku-ku, tokyo

c.m.